CHILD SEXUAL ABUSE
Hope for Healing

Maxine Hancock
& Karen Burton Mains

Child
Sexual Abuse

HOPE
FOR
HEALING

Revised Edition

Harold Shaw Publishers
Wheaton, Illinois

Contents

Acknowledgments

Our debts in writing and updating a book like this are, of course, many. Our special thanks go to the many survivors to whom we have talked, or who wrote to tell us of their experiences, and especially to the four who shared so wholly out of their lives: "Kathy," "Rita," "Margaret," and "George." These names are invented and some details slightly altered to protect the identities of those who have told us their stories. The many "voices" quoted throughout the book are actual quotations from letters received or interviews conducted.

The book has a special debt to Audrey McRonald— "Kathy"—who first asked us to write this book and whose story serves as the backbone of this book. Audrey now conducts an extensive awareness-raising and counseling ministry called "Hope for the Abused." The address of this ministry may be found with the resources listed at the end of this book.

As we sought to understand the effects of child sexual abuse, we consulted with experts in the field. Early drafts of the manuscript were reviewed by sexual assault counselors and psychotherapists, as well as by abuse survivors. Valuable observations and insights offered by these readers were taken into consideration in drafting the final work, and we are grateful for their input.

In preparing this revised edition, we have had additional input from many readers and the valuable assistance of researcher Isabel Calhoun Farrar, to whom we are especially grateful. At Harold Shaw Publishers, editor Mary Horner Collins has coordinated the revisions and kept the project on track.

To all, our thanks.

Introduction

When Karen Mains and I joined forces several years ago to write a book for women wounded by the experience of child sexual abuse, we could not have foreseen how eagerly the book would be welcomed. We also could not have guessed how wide and deep was the need for it. We were simply responding to the voices of women who cried out to be heard, to be understood, to be healed. Now, with written and spoken thanks from hundreds of women on several continents to encourage us (the book is now being published in several languages as well as English), we are both glad and sad to present an updated edition. We are glad to continue this handmaidenly ministry to our sisters and to the Christian community. We are sad that the book continues to be desperately needed, both to inform the church about child sexual abuse and to support survivors of child sexual abuse in their long walk into wholeness.

Writing this book took us out of our own comfort zones. In our separate ministries as authors and speakers, Karen and I had addressed hundreds of gatherings of women across a wide spectrum of church denominations. We heard countless stories of child sexual abuse from women, and their repeated plea: "Someone, please, speak on our behalf from within the Christian community." And so, not as professional counselors or abuse survivors, but as listeners and speakers, we felt it laid upon us to reveal, to explain, to comfort, to encourage, to be agents for healing.

In this process of listening and learning, we took a dark pilgrimage into awareness. We went through our own traumas of shock, disbelief, and anger as we reviewed the findings of researchers, talked to sexual assault counselors, and listened to survivors (and, most painfully, also to their abusers). We have wept at the devastation that comes from the violation of children. At the same time, we have also shared in a fellowship of courageous and triumphant women. The stories of those who had truly experienced healing, coupled with the scriptural basis for such healing, gave us hope that even this great evil is included in the triumph of love and healing over evil and destruction.

We have written this book for three groups of readers. First, for women survivors of child sexual abuse. We are aware that male children, too, are abused. However, our experience, our reading in the research literature, and our in-depth interviews all concern themselves with women who were abused as children. This book is intended to help these women understand why and how the abuse has affected them so deeply and to offer them a path toward healing.

Second, we have written for those who, without the experience of child sexual abuse themselves, seek to be informed in order to support women on their long walk into wholeness after the shattering experience of abuse. These supporters of survivors may be lay or pastoral counselors, family members, or caring friends.

Finally, we have written to inform and equip the Christian church as a whole to understand and attack this evil at its roots. We believe that evil flourishes in the darkness. Hence, the better informed Christians are, the greater the chance that the church can take a stand against all that would feed or hide this evil, and offer genuine support and understanding to survivors. It is our hope that we will join holy hands and lift holy prayers against sexual practices that threaten our wholeness individually and as a culture. We must work together to denounce all forms of sexual exploitation of the weak by the strong, and the evil that feeds such actions—pornography.

While the book was not written specifically to inform professional counselors, it has been used widely as a counseling tool. We have included suggested action plans under the heading "Something You Can Do Right Now." By using these action plans within a structure allowing for accountability and discussion, a woman survivor and her counselor (or friend or spouse or support group) can use the book as an interactive workbook. Many have found this to be a most helpful aspect of this book.

We are convinced that women who have suffered child sexual abuse need advocates—many of them. We believe that the church, when it honors its calling to be a nonsexualized fellowship of brothers and sisters within a sexually polarized culture, is uniquely equipped to bring healing, through both community and liturgy. We worship a transcendent God whose eternal nature as "I AM" is beyond gender assignation; we also believe that Jesus of Nazareth is still woman's greatest Advocate and Healer.

For you, the woman survivor, may this book be a tool of liberation and comfort, encouraging the healing process to begin and instilling hope. We pray that as you read you will experience the tender love and acceptance of One whose grace is great enough to heal the most damaged hearts and emotions, whose love and power can bring order, dignity, and purpose out of blackest chaos.

This Jesus, whom as Christians we affirm to be God's Anointed One, the Christ, stood beside the tomb long ago and spoke gently to an anguished, grieving woman. By his Spirit, he still stands beside the weeping women of this generation in the mourning places of their lives and asks, "Woman, why are you weeping? Whom are you seeking?"

Christ is present, if we only can recognize him, at the death scenes of our pasts. He is able to heal the memories, roll away the gravestones that seal in all our pain, and speak our names so we can look up and see that the garden-green resurrection day is dawning.

Our prayer is that you will meet this Jesus, this God-sent One who is able to make you whole.

Maxine Hancock
Karen Burton Mains

1
The Nature of Child Sexual Abuse

Kathy's Story

"Kathy" is a professional woman with a wide range of abilities. Besides being trained as a psychiatric nurse, she is a loving wife and mother who skillfully manages her home. Kathy experienced both the pain of sexual abuse and the joy of healing. She shares her story with us.

My childhood was very normal until I was about five years of age. Beginning at the age of five and continuing until I was almost twelve, I was sexually abused by an uncle who lived close by, who was almost like a big brother to me. He was nineteen when it started. I trusted him then; it was fun to be with him. He used to take me around with him—a very big deal to a five-year-old.

All of this developed gradually. He started taking me to the barn to be alone with him. Later, he began to fondle me and expose himself to me, and ask me to kiss and handle him. I knew within myself that this wasn't right, but he kept telling me that this was our secret and that I wasn't ever to tell anybody. He promised he would never hurt me. It is true that he was never violent or angry. It was always "in love," so to speak.

Even though I knew it was somehow wrong, I was afraid to say anything or to go to anybody about it. But as years went on, his handling of me became more and more aggressive.

At some point during those years, I attempted to tell my mother. I don't really remember what I said, but I was not able to make her understand. She knew I had grown to dislike this particular uncle. She may have denied the reason, or perhaps I failed to communicate the reality to her. Anyhow, it became a closed door between us.

The abuse finally stopped when my family moved away from the farm and I no longer had any contact with my uncle. When we made a return visit a year or so later, he again tried to attack me. But I was able to resist. I was old enough then and very afraid. I realized that I did have some rights.

It's strange, isn't it? As a child you feel like you don't have any right to question what an adult is doing. You are brought up to respect adults and think that they know what is best. I found myself saying, "Well, I guess it must be O.K. . . . He's a grown-up."

———————

Child sexual abuse. Finally we have a name for the unspeakable, the unthinkable. For too long, survivors of child sexual abuse have lived in a suffocating darkness of silence. There were no words with which to name their wounds, no ears to hear their cries.

Now at last we are hearing their stories. Their pain is reaching out and touching our own nerves. Kathy's true story, which we will follow from abuse to recovery, is typical. She is one of thousands of women who must be heard. We will begin to hear their voices in this book, and then, if we listen, we will begin to recognize them all around us.

I didn't realize the extent of abuse in America—I have felt so alone with this problem.

———————

When my sisters and I were growing up, sexually abused

*by our stepfather, we didn't realize that we were a few
statistic points in a large and growing population.*

---

*Some years ago, memories I thought were buried sur-
faced anew. About this same time the media began to
explore and report on the subject of incest. Would you
believe it was not until then that I really knew what the
word meant and that I was a victim?*

Despite the overwhelming evidence that child sexual abuse
may still be an under-reported crime, we all must fight a strong
desire to deny or avoid this subject.[1] Survivors wish they could
forget about it but know that they cannot. Most of those who
have not felt the pain simply prefer not to deal with information about child sexual abuse.

Moving from ignorance to awareness is a costly step. After
a meeting in which I (Maxine) had spoken about child sexual
abuse, a young woman came to talk with me, identifying herself as an incest survivor. "I almost didn't come tonight," she
said. "When anything about incest comes on the television, I
switch channels or get out of the room. It's just too painful.
But now I know I have to face my past."

We can understand her struggle with avoidance, even denial. As we have researched this subject, we have gone through
an emotional progression from shock and horror to terrible
anger and then into deep grief. Finally, out of that grief has
come the determination to speak and to act.

What Constitutes Child Sexual Abuse?

*I should have sought help sooner, but in my ignorance as
to what constitutes abuse, I never saw it as such and so
was unaware of the root of my misery.*

Many survivors ask, "Was I abused? Am I a victim?" They
are not alone in being unsure as to what constitutes sexual
abuse. Even professional sources don't agree on the specific
definitions regarding child sexual abuse.[2]

Let's spell it out.

Child sexual abuse covers a broad range of sexually-oriented activities that involve the child. These range from sexual exposure and fondling all the way to anal or vaginal penetration. The following activities are considered to be sexually abusive:

- an adult showing a child his/her genitals
- an adult asking a child to undress to be looked at or fondled
- an adult touching a child's genitals
- an adult having a child touch his/her genitals
- oral-genital contact
- forced masturbation
- digital penetration, or penetration of anus or vagina with another object
- anal penetration
- intercourse
- use of children for the production of pornographic materials

Some researchers also include verbal sexual propositions, remarks, or jokes.[3] Sexual abuse of children consists of activities that expose children to sexual stimulation inappropriate to their age, psychological development, and role in the family.

When such activities occur between family members, the terms *incest* or *intrafamilial child sexual abuse* are applied. Psychologist Juliann Whetsell-Mitchell broadly defines incest as sexual activity on the part of "one or more persons who derive authority through ongoing emotional bonding with that child. . . . Therefore, incest could include anyone with whom the child has established an emotional relationship. This is a much broader definition of incest than has been given in the past."[4]

Most researchers apply the term *incest* somewhat more exclusively than Whetsell-Mitchell, but still include not only blood relatives but also adults who live in a family relationship to the child: stepfathers, stepbrothers, stepgrandparents. Figure 1.1 shows the various approaches to defining incest.

Child sexual abuse which is perpetrated by someone outside

Definitions of Incest

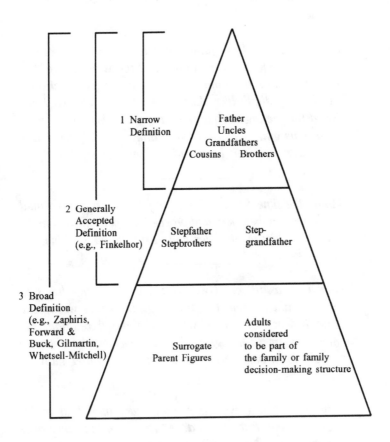

Figure 1.1

Various definitions of the term *incest* exist in research literature. Narrowly used, the term refers to sexual activities between blood relatives. Broadly used, it includes sexual activities initiated by any adult who plays the role of a family member in the life of the child. The broader definition is becoming generally accepted.

of the family—a babysitter, family friend, or unknown molester—is termed *extrafamilial child sexual abuse.*

Do these things really happen? Hear a few of the voices we have heard:

> *As a small child my father initiated "secret" meetings with me. He touched me in places I felt were wrong, but he said it was a "game." He also made me touch him in places I didn't like. As time went on I realized I enjoyed the feeling despite the guilt. . . . I have lived with enormous guilt because I was willing to take part in this sin. I don't know if I am truly a "victim."*

> *About the time I was thirteen or fourteen, my dad would come into my bedroom and proceed to "pet" me and make me "pet" him. Night after night I'd pray he wouldn't.*

> *When I was fifteen, I was raped by my stepfather and had a child by him. I kept telling him it was wrong; he said it was not, as he was not a blood relation. My mother went to her grave blaming me, but he ought to have known better as he was forty years older than I.*

> *My brother, who was four years older than I, shared a bed with me. Enough said? As time went on other boys were invited into "fun" situations. I can remember one time when there were several boys taking turns.*

> *I was molested by a babysitter when I was three or four. When I was nine, I was raped by my sixteen-year-old brother and sold to his friends.*

> *I was a victim of statutory rape when I was twelve years old, although I believe that something probably hap-*

*pened to me in the area of abuse long before it culmi-
nated in the sexual act.*

---

*As a little girl I was a victim of sexual fondling by a
much older cousin. Though this cousin used all of his
younger girl cousins in this way, our families did nothing
but tell us to keep away from him.*

---

*I was sexually stimulated as a baby so very early in life
that I craved sexual stimulation.*

My first sexual experience was at age four.

---

*I was sexually abused by my father from the time when
I was a very tiny child until I began dating. . . . I was
brought up to obey my parents and felt there must be
something wrong with me. My younger sister also recently confessed to being sexually abused.*

The real horror of these stories is that the great majority of
those who are sexually abused experience the abuse from
someone they know and trust. And unlike sexual molestation,
which is often a sudden and forceful event, intrafamilial child
sexual abuse is usually continued over a long period of time.
The child's trust has been gained only to be betrayed. Sexual
activity often begins with a subtle progression from normal
loving touch to sexual fondling. The child, naturally confused,
often accepts the authority of the adult as warrant that the
activity is either all right or unavoidable. Sandra Butler writes:

Needs for human contact and warmth become translated
into the specific sexual form of [a] father's stroking and
fondling. In a home in which the only love and tenderness a girl receives takes the form of sexual play, the
child's slowly growing sense of the wrongness of such

intimacy takes years to surface and, when it does, is coupled with her own incorporated feelings of guilt and responsibility for having let it go on.[5]

Kathy's story illustrates very clearly what Alexander G. Zaphiris, who has conducted intensive research in the causes and effects of incest, calls "the conditioning phase," in which the child is gradually conditioned to accept an adult's sexual behavior as "part and parcel of love and affection."[6] Counselor Dan B. Allender calls this phase "Stage 1" of an abuser's typical strategy: "the development of intimacy and secrecy." He writes, "The essence of Stage 1 is the offer of relationship, intimacy, special privilege, and rewards. It can be viewed as the offer of water to a person dying of thirst."[7]

How Common Is Child Sexual Abuse?

"Living in a small rural community," a police officer states, "I am aware that many of our citizens choose to believe that child abuse couldn't or doesn't happen here. It is this kind of thinking that allows child abuse to flourish." How many people are affected by child sexual abuse? Every year more and more child sexual abuse cases are being reported to authorities.[8] And it's likely that reported cases represent only the tip of the iceberg.

Children tend to keep their sexual abuse experiences secret (for reasons discussed in chapter 2, Figure 2.2). Therefore, most knowledge about the incidence of child sexual abuse must be gained from adults recalling experiences that occurred in their childhoods. Obviously, there are some difficulties with accuracy and detail with this form of reporting; but researchers discovered that based on recall, one in five to one in three of the females surveyed reported they had experienced undesired sexual activity as children.[9]

One of the most comprehensive national studies to date was authored by Finkelhor, Hotaling, Lewis, and Smith (1990) (see Figure 1.2). Looking at their conclusions, we find that: 27% of the 1,374 women surveyed reported an experience of sexual abuse before the age of eighteen and 23% of the women who reported being abused stated that the abuse occurred before the age of eight.[10]

Three Landmark Studies of Incidence[11]			
Date	*Researcher*	*Sample*	*% of Sample Reporting Sexual Abuse*
1990	Finkelhor, Hotaling, Lewis, Smith	1,374 women across U.S.	27% (before age 18) Contact and noncontact abuse
1992	Elliot and Briere	2,963 professional women across U.S.	27% (before age 16) Contact abuse only
1994	Wilsnack, Klassen, Vogeltanz, Harris	1,099 women (oversample of heavy drinkers)	23% (before age 18) Contact and forced exposure and exhibition

Figure 1.2

Perpetrator Characteristics[13]		
Avg. Age (years)	35	
Sex		
Male	90%	*Most perpetrators of sexual abuse are male*
Female	10%	
Relationship to Involved Children		
Family	29%	
Not Family but known to Child	60%	
Stranger	11%	*Only 11% of perpetrators are strangers to the child*

Figure 1.3

Who Are the Perpetrators?

Fathers. Stepfathers. Uncles. Brothers. Cousins. Trusted family friends. The nice man next door. In at least 89 percent of child sexual abuse cases the perpetrator is someone the child loves and knows.[12] Figure 1.3 shows what is known about sexual abusers.

Sick, sordid, unspeakably selfish, the perpetrators of child sexual abuse exploit the innocence and trust of young children for their own sexual gratification. We will take a closer look at various profiles of the abuse perpetrator in chapters 10 and 11.

Are Church Families Exempt?

Sadly, we have to concur with the mounting evidence that child sexual abuse also occurs within church-oriented homes. Being in a family that is "religious," even "evangelical" or "fundamental," does not guarantee a youngster protection from sexual abuse. In fact, studies indicate that child sexual abuse occurs at almost the same rate of incidence in all levels of society.

Psychotherapist Carolyn Holderread Heggen maintains that conservative religiosity combined with traditional role beliefs is the second-best predictor of child sexual abuse—second only after the use of drugs or alcohol by the father. Heggen lists six prominent conservative beliefs among child sexual abusers:

(1) God intends for men to dominate and women and children to submit.
(2) Because of her role in the Fall, woman is morally inferior to man.
(3) Children are inherently evil and must have their wills broken.
(4) Marriages must be preserved at all cost.
(5) Suffering is a Christian virtue.
(6) Christians must promptly forgive those who sin against them.[14]

Although some of these beliefs may seem to be consistent

with some traditional readings of Scripture, none should ever lead to abuse within the family—especially incest, which is explicitly condemned in the Bible. Richard Butman, clinical psychologist and professor of psychology, writes: "Despite the clear prohibition of incest in Leviticus 6–18, the majority of reported aggressors are regular church attenders. It is difficult to measure someone's 'Christianity,' but researchers do report that the adult males tend to be very devout, moralistic, and conservative in their religious beliefs."[15]

We need to confront the reality that all "religious" rationalizations of abuse are worked out from deeply internalized beliefs that a man, because he is male, should have what he desires—at whatever cost to others; that a man in some sense "owns" his wife and children and has proprietary claim to their lives and bodies. When the church refuses to endorse male privilege as a scripturally sanctioned norm, it will cut the ground out from under rationalizations of abusers.

Beliefs such as those listed by Heggen in items 1, 2, and 3, while deeply rooted in some traditions of biblical interpretation, ignore the clear teaching of Scripture that all of humanity is equally fallen and all are equally redeemed through faith in the Lord Jesus Christ as Savior (see, for example, Romans 3:23-26). Male domination is nowhere *prescribed*, but rather *described* as an outcome of the Fall. In fact, the premise of male domination is destroyed by Jesus' call to mutual love and service. The New Testament call to wifely submission is balanced by the call to husbandly self-sacrifice, radically subverting any attempt to justify male dominance, domination, or privilege. In fact, Jesus absolutely repudiates anything that looks like a hierarchy in which one "lords it" over another (see Matthew 20:27).

Beliefs 4, 5, and 6 in Heggen's list are somewhat more problematic, since each contains a measure of truth that may be twisted to support or hide abuse. While without doubt the Bible upholds the sacredness of marriage and the seriousness of covenant keeping, a prior concern for the well-being of persons over the stability of structures is everywhere evident in the teaching of the New Testament. No woman should feel she must stay in a marriage in which her own well-being or that of her children is threatened by a physically or sexually abusive husband. And for anyone to use the beliefs that suffering produces character or that Christian victims must automatically offer forgiveness in order to rationalize abuse, is an obvious and almost unthinkable perversion of Scripture.[16]

The voices we have listened to speak from within the church as well as from the wider community:

> *I am sixty-one years old, but when I was grade-school aged I was molested by a family adult who was a young minister of about twenty-two years of age.*

> *Having been sexually abused by my father—in a so-called Christian home—for a period of approximately seven years, you can imagine some of the difficulty and confusion that I've experienced throughout my life (I am forty-three years old now).*

> *Are there any normal Christian families? When my two oldest girls were in their teens, their grandfather, a faithful church member, was putting his hands where they never should be. He showed the girls pornographic material. He paid another girl to let him "feel." He remains in everyone's memory as a "great pillar of the church."*

> *After telling of incestuous experiences as a child, a woman says, "I should add that my father is a Christian and I was raised in a good evangelical church which we attended faithfully."*

The problem exists. Because we want it to go away does not mean that it will go away. Our very silence allows it to grow to horrifying proportions. Abused children all too frequently become adults who abuse their own children. The sins of the father are being visited upon the children. Silence will not help survivors pick up the pieces of long-term sexual problems, wretched self-images, or severe personality disorders. Nor will silence confront the guilty with their need for confession, forgiveness, and redemption. Two things need to be broken—first our long, uneasy silence; then, as a consequence, the cycle of sexual abuse.

The church, empowered by the living Christ, is able to offer healing through supportive, loving community only when we lose our fear of walking into the hell of pain-filled lives so that the abused as well as the abuser can be set free.

This is our assignment: To hear each other's stories. To feel each other's pain. With divine power and help, to set each other free.

So help us, God.

2
The Physical and Emotional Aftermath

Kathy's Story

After I was ten or so, I thought a lot about what my uncle and I did together. The sexual activity seemed to have developed into a need within me. It became something I hated and yet something that, in spite of myself, I almost looked forward to. In time, I felt I was as much responsible for what was happening as he was. I had a lot of inner guilt because a part of me enjoyed the stimulation.

I felt that I was different from other children, living in a world of my own. I felt as if I had never really been a child. It seemed I had been plunged into an adult world and I never did the normal things that kids around me did. Naturally I wondered: *What is different about me? Why does he do this to me? Is there something wrong with me that makes him choose me?*

When my parents moved and the whole affair came to a sudden stop, I developed an intense hatred for my uncle. I felt that he had ruined my life, leaving me nothing worth living for. Many, many times I thought about how I might kill him. I thought that if I could just get him off the face of the earth, maybe I could forget about the whole thing.

Throughout my teenage years, I was suicidal. If I couldn't

get rid of him, I felt the next best thing was to get rid of myself. I thought about killing myself many times and actually attempted suicide when I was seventeen. I took an overdose of sleeping pills and ended up in the hospital for a couple of weeks. That only made me feel worse about myself.

Having been exposed to sex at such an early age, I had intense sexual struggles. The drives that were a part of normal adolescence were, for me, explosive, creating tremendous conflict for me. I dated a lot during my teens, using dating situations as a way to get back at men. I had no respect for males. Period. I knew you couldn't trust them, knew they were only looking for one thing, knew they were users. So I used them and abused them. For me, dating was a chance to play a game of torment, arousing my partner as much as possible and then rebuffing him short of going all the way. At the same time, of course, I was tormenting myself.

Meanwhile I managed to maintain my studies. I made good grades in school and went into nursing, hoping that I would discover something that would help me understand how to overcome what I was struggling with. The courses I enjoyed most were psychology and sociology; but although I studied them intensely and read everything I could find in the library, I still couldn't find anything that could help me.

Increasingly, life became a struggle. I wanted to live just one day of my life without thinking about my past or without having it affect me. That's all I wanted—one day without flashbacks or horrible memories, just one day without anger and hatred consuming me.

The whole thing seemed too horrible to tell anybody. I wanted to talk with someone many times. But then I would think, "It all happened so long ago—what's the point of saying anything about it now?" Even when a psychiatrist talked with me after my attempted suicide, I wouldn't tell him the whole story.

I was nearly twenty-six before I met a man I felt I could actually trust, a very kind and loving man. Despite my emotional problems during nursing training, I had achieved my professional goals and was an established and respected psychiatric nurse. I longed for a home and family, but although

I knew I really cared for this man, I was very afraid of marriage, uncertain as to whether I was capable of loving a man with constancy. So I literally entered marriage with a clearly defined escape clause. If it didn't work, I decided, I would just have to get a divorce.

At first our sexual relationship was difficult—very guarded, very tense. Much as I cared for my husband, I still found the physical relationship difficult. Frequently, flashbacks interfered. I began to think that if I didn't change in my response to him, I would lose him. So with grit and determination, I literally exerted mind over matter, determined to overcome that problem.

We had some happy years; the birth of our first son thrilled us, and I was very much wrapped up in this new life. Although I was still struggling daily, I was coping. Anyone looking at me from the outside would not have guessed that I was having difficulty. Even my husband had no idea of the past that still shadowed me.

Kathy's story illustrates many of the most commonly reported long-term struggles of child sexual abuse victims. The word *survivor* is an apt description for those who live with an abusive past. Like survivors of other life-changing traumas, many carry scars inflicted on them by the actions of other people for the rest of their lives.

We need to really listen to the stories of these survivors and begin to map out what psychotherapist Susan Forward calls "the emotional geography of incest."[1] Such a map can, in turn, help abuse survivors identify characteristics of the terrain they traverse in their own pilgrimage toward wholeness and recovery.

Because our sources, and those reporting to other researchers, are nearly all women, we will speak of survivors in the feminine gender. However, the dynamics which operate so disruptively apply to male victims of child sexual abuse as well. (There is a growing sense among researchers that sexual abuse of male children is very much underreported, and that the ratio of male to female victims may be as high as three to five.[2])

There are, of course, dissenting voices within society that pose the question, "What's wrong with adult/child sex?" Some organized groups lobby to promote pedophilia as a lifestyle. (A pedophile is someone, usually male, who has a strong sexual interest in children.) Such groups as the North American Man/Boy Love Association (NAMBLA) urge that the age of consent should be lowered to four years of age. The notorious René Guyon Society, based in southern California, has a motto of "Sex before age eight, or else it's too late." Internet addresses include usernets focused on adult/child sex.

While these groups are small in membership, they are active in lobbying at state and federal levels for changes in laws relating to children and sex. For those of us who have worked with and listened to survivors of incest and other forms of child sexual abuse, the possibility that serious attention is being given to ideas that would strip children of even the very minimal existing legal protection can only evoke horror.

Ask Somebody Who's Been Through It

In *Kiss Daddy Goodnight*, Louise Armstrong reports on her own and others' experiences of incest. Her answer to the question, "What's wrong with it?" is frank and blunt: "Oh, god. Tell them to ask somebody who's been through it."[3]

As Florence Rush states in *The Best Kept Secret*, "Once we perceive, question, and challenge the existence of the sexual abuse of children, we have taken the first crucial step toward the elimination of the degradation, humiliation, and corrosion of our most valuable human resource—our young."[4]

It is, of course, difficult to establish absolute cause-and-effect relationships between child sexual abuse and the many problems that survivors experience and attribute to it. "I know I blamed *everything* that happened to me on the incest in my childhood," a young woman told us. Some researchers have noted that child sexual abuse becomes a central focus around which negative experiences and emotions cluster.[5] But there is overwhelming evidence that a childhood sexual experience with an older person is negative and damaging, causing "the issues that are found in all our lives [to be] more intensely and dramatically present in the struggles of those who have been sexually abused."[6] The aftereffects may vary in intensity and severity, but they are common to most who have experienced child sexual abuse.

As examples of the personal pain and turmoil which may exist even in those who seem to have made an adequate adjustment to life, Researchers Brandt Steele and Helen Alexander list the following:

- feelings of inferiority
- nonintegrated personality
- poor basic trust
- repressed anger
- unresolved identifications and fixations
- difficulties in establishing and maintaining relationships
- sexual dysfunction and/or aberrant sexual behaviors
- shame, guilt, and fear of social disapproval
- underlying feelings of helplessness and fear[7]

Such a litany of pain is authenticated by many researchers. It is echoed by many of the women whose stories we have listened to. And their stories are even more convincing than the statistical data. Child sexual abuse almost always is related to deep and lasting pain which may affect every aspect of life: physical, emotional, relational, and spiritual. One person put it this way: "At age thirty-five and a wife and mother, I am experiencing pain, anger, and confusion as a result of being an incest survivor and later, a rape victim. I feel flayed to the core of my spirit."

Let us examine the various areas of a person's life that lie under the shadow of child sexual abuse. (Figure 2.1 shows one way of understanding the links between some of the long-term effects of abuse.)

Physical Problems Resulting from Abuse

The possible immediate physical consequences of child sexual abuse are spelled out by Dr. Marvin Blumberg. They range from feeding and sleeping disturbances in infants and toddlers to bed-wetting in young school-age children, and such gynecological disturbances as dysmenorrhea (painful menstrual periods) in adolescent girls. Vulvar lacerations, abrasions in the genital region, and, occasionally, venereal and other sexually transmitted infections may result from sexual contact.

In adolescence, abuse may result in pregnancy, leading either to childbirth or abortion, both highly traumatic for a teenage girl. But the immediate physical effects are often only a prelude to lingering physical problems.

> *I wonder if the very early and rough treatment I experienced had anything to do with my periods never being normal.*

> *I have been treated for premenstrual syndrome, which my doctor links to the child sexual abuse I experienced.*

Kathy, the nurse whose continuing story we will follow through the early chapters of this book, is under observation for possible cervical cancer after abnormal cells showed up on a routine Pap smear. "If after all I have suffered, I should have to pay for my uncle's sin in this way, too, I don't know how I will handle it," she says. She knows that frequent early intercourse can be a predisposing factor in the incidence of cervical cancer.

The Emotional Geography of Incest[8]

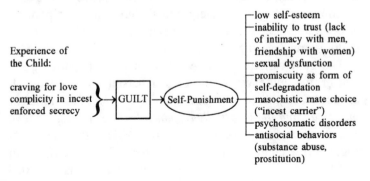

Figure 2.1

Some of our sources cite obesity as a response to sexual abuse. Psychiatrist Karin C. Meiselman speculates that there may be a link between obesity and incestuous experiences, although her research sample was not large enough for any definitive conclusions.[9] Since being overweight may make a woman less attractive, it can serve as a means of withdrawing from sexual activity, a sort of protective covering up for the person. One women notes, "After early sexual activity with my brother and his friends, I became very overweight. I am actually surprised to find myself married. I didn't think I would ever find anyone who could love a fat person."

The paradoxical craving for love/withdrawal from intimacy is evident in her statement. Researchers also see other eating disorders such as anorexia and especially bulimia as long-term effects of child sexual abuse. Because their only experiences of intimacy in childhood were sexual in nature, some survivors of child sexual abuse believe that keeping their bodies trim and attractive is their only hope for intimacy with others.[10]

Besides these specific physical problems, many abuse survivors experience psychosomatic disorders such as migraines, stomach and skin problems, and disabling aches and pains.

Emotional Problems Associated with Abuse

1. *Guilt.* Over and over again, the theme of guilt shows up in the survivors' stories. Tremendous guilt is carried by survivors who wonder how they could have let the whole thing continue without telling someone. They have been locked into a sort of conspiracy against society, urged, threatened, or perhaps bribed into silence. They have, however reluctantly, shared a guilty secret (see Figure 2.2).

The guilt carried by survivors is partly an imparted guilt, laid on the abuse victim by another person's wrongdoing. It cannot be emphasized too strongly that *no child has sufficient understanding to be sexually responsible*. The craving for love and attention that renders a child vulnerable is the natural response of a child to trusted adults in her life. The abuse of that trust is the responsibility of the adult who initiates sexual activity. The unequal distribution of power between abuser and abused throws the weight of responsibility on the adult involved. Nonetheless, the real horror of sexual abuse lies in the fact that sexual activity is a shared experience, and the victim is stained with the guilt of it.

2. *Shame.* Accompanying the overwhelming guilt is the feeling of shame. Women express it in words like these:

I still feel so dirty and unloved, wondering why my husband wants me.

I was molested and raped as a child of eleven years. . . . All my life I have felt dirty and worthless and no good.

At eighteen I left home to go to a university, still feeling unclean and unworthy, a six-foot brick wall around me.

The hardest thing of all to accept is that the victim is innocent (even though she feels guilty) and deserves to be freed from the consequences of abuse.

Why Victims Don't Tell[11]

Mary Ellen Siemers (1986) summarized the reasons reported by researchers for a general reluctance on the part of abuse victims to share their secret with others:

- Loyalty and love for the abuser make it nearly impossible for them to speak up against people who are supposed to be their protectors, comforters, and closest friends.
- When they do get up enough courage to tell someone, the listener may respond to their revelations with horror, disbelief, judgment, or denial.
- The victim is often passive because of a perception of the abuser's authority; the young child often being told that the sexual activity is acceptable but must be kept secret.
- Real or implied threats are often sufficient to secure passive cooperation and secrecy in the absence of any reasonable alternatives.
- The severity of laws against abusers may increase the ambivalence and fearfulness of incest victims to seek help outside the family.
- They tell no one simply because no one asks.

Figure 2.2

This sense of shame seems to be rooted in the experience of being physically overpowered and coerced into activities which are often repugnant to the child. In his book *The Wounded Heart,* Dan Allender explains the role of shame in child sexual abuse:

> Consider the damage done to the soul when the abuse is fused with the legitimate longings of the heart. The flower of deep longing for love is somehow hideously intertwined with the weed of abuse. Longings are wed to abuse, abuse begets shame, and shame is inextricably related to a hatred for one's own hungry soul.[12]

In this way, survivors link being forced into distasteful activities with their cravings for love; thus they become ashamed of their longings.

3. *Lack of Self-Worth and Learned Passivity.* Survivors speak of, and often demonstrate, a low sense of self-esteem, a sad and often crippling loss of self-worth as a result of sexual abuse as children.

> *I think I must be a very dumb person because as a child I thought I had to do what everyone wanted me to do. . . . And to this day I have a hard time saying no to people and not letting them take advantage of me.*

This lack of self-worth often leads to the development of a learned "victim mentality." In *Turning Fear to Hope,* Holly Wagner Green explains the phenomenon of learned passivity:

> Counselor Lenore Walker describes experiments in which laboratory animals and human volunteers were confined and then exposed to random, painful stimuli over which they had no control and from which they could not escape. Once they realized their behavior had no effect on what happened to them, their motivation to help themselves seemed to die. They ceased trying to get away or gain relief, actually ignoring obvious avenues of escape, even when these were pointed out. When they

had learned they were powerless, they stopped struggling and became passive.[13]

Victims of abuse have also been exposed to random pain which could not be escaped. Many of you who are reading this book were victims in the past; that past still victimizes you. You need to have someone stand next to you, to hear someone say, "There is hope. *You can be helped.* Hundreds of others before you have sought help and found it. The power of Christ can reach into all the abnormalities and perversions that humans can devise and make things right. I believe this because I have seen it happen. It can happen to you."

4. *Anger and Hatred that Lead to Depression and Despair.* An enormous anger burns in many survivors. Quite rightly, they feel defrauded.

> *The intensity of my anger is brutal and potentially self-destructive.*

> *Thank you that I can be angry. . . . I think I can finally start to live. I can look people in the face. And if I want to be angry at the injustice of sexual abuse, I'll be angry. And if anyone doesn't like it, that's fine.*

The tragedy of anger is that it very often turns inward on the survivor, resulting in depression, despair, and suicidal thoughts or actions. Sometimes, too, it erupts in irrational fury directed toward a husband or children. Anger and hatred always use up the energy survivors need to get on with their lives. In her autobiographical book *Daddy's Girl,* Charlotte Vale Allen puts it this way: "Hating takes up so much energy, so much concentration, that there's very little left to do anything else."[14]

5. *Fearfulness and Anxiety.* Once the strong sense of basic trust has been betrayed, many survivors experience fearfulness and anxiety. Often these fears are overwhelming. Free-floating, unfocused anxiety is something that many survivors live with. Women tell us about this general feeling of fearfulness:

My sister and I were abused as children. It has been extremely hard to overcome fears that stemmed from my past.

At age three I was molested by a man who held me on his lap. I guess I was too young to really understand exactly what was happening, but I wonder if it didn't have some effect on me. I grew into a fearful, shy, and mistrusting child, characteristics that lasted into my adult life.

With my father disliking me and my older stepbrother abusing me sexually, I felt I couldn't trust God or anyone else. My life was full of fears.

For some, the fears erupt at particular moments in relationships, shadowing some of the most joyous events and stages of life.

I was sexually assaulted by my father throughout adolescence. I hated—hated—hated it. When I married I thought I had the past licked. Then, when my sons became handsome teenagers I became terrified of showing them affection for fear I would feel toward them what my dad had felt toward me.

When I was pregnant, my husband wanted a girl, and suddenly I felt these unwarranted fears that my husband would do the same things to my daughter that my father had done to me.

For numbers of survivors there is a special fear of intimacy, of letting anyone close. This fearfulness is often particularly directed toward males who are all perceived as possible betrayers. Obviously such anxiety inhibits friendships, short-changes and fragments marriages, and sometimes results in overprotective parenting. And, of course, it impedes faith, making the spiritual pilgrimage of the abuse survivor especially difficult.

3
Behavioral and Relational Problems

Kathy's Story

Our second son was born two years later. As the pressures increased with two small children, it became more and more difficult to cope with what I was feeling. The summer I was expecting our third child, I reached a new low. Once again I became suicidal. Every day I would think of ways to kill myself—and then I would check myself, feeling that it would be unfair to leave my husband with two babies. Then I would think that maybe I should kill all three of us and leave my husband free. Time after time I would put the two little boys in the car and drive at absolutely crazy speeds, hoping that we would all be killed.

One morning during that summer when I was pregnant with our daughter, I woke up with an overwhelming desire to die. I dressed the two boys and went out to the car again. This time, I thought, I would drive the car off a cliff. But again, as I drove toward my destination, I felt, *Oh, I can't do this!*

I remembered a friend whom I had known since my early teens. I knew she was a Christian, and suddenly I thought that perhaps she could help me. I turned around and drove to her house, only to find no one at home. It was as though my one ray of hope had been wiped out.

Crying and desperate, I stumbled back from her door to the car. I knew that somehow I had to get help. I had to let somebody know what was going on inside me. I drove the car to the plaza, went into a department store, and began to steal as much as I could shove into my purse. In my distraught condition, I reasoned that if I did something bizarre enough—like shoplifting when I had lots of money in my purse and every credit card you could ask for—I would get help. The court, I thought, would surely appoint a psychiatrist.

But what happened was both more and less than what I had expected. As I left the store, I was apprehended by a security guard and taken back into the store while the police were called. Then I was taken to the police station and put into a holding cell—I and my two little boys. I was charged, fingerprinted, and finally released. When my court appearance came, I went to court alone, refusing to get a lawyer. I just wanted to be punished—and perhaps, helped.

But as it turned out, the court could not have cared less about me as a person. Not a single question was asked. I was declared guilty as charged. I paid the fine and was released, worse off than I had been before. I had only added guilt to guilt.

———

As we have seen, the inner suffering experienced by survivors of child sexual abuse has its own geography. But the damage done by the abuse reaches beyond the inner emotional life of the survivor, like a hated hand shadowing all behavior patterns and relationships.

> *I spent a lot of time running away when I got older, but I never found anyone I could trust enough to tell why I kept running away, why I didn't want to go home. I didn't feel like I should live.*

———

> *Men and women who have been sexually abused are chained in their hearts, minds, emotions, in their destructive lifestyles. . . . (I was molested and raped as a child*

of eleven and I've been into drugs, drinking, etc.)

For survivors, understanding why they feel and act the way they do, and why they may have difficulty in establishing and maintaining relationships, may be an important step toward healing. In this chapter, we will look first at what seem to be the reasons for such wide-ranging damage to the whole person, and then at behavioral and relational problems which survivors commonly experience.

Roots of Pain

There is no doubt that child sexual abuse is a deeply damaging experience for the victim. We have already looked at some of the long-term problems that survivors have to struggle with. It would seem that the damage may stem from some or all of the following factors:

1. *Betrayal of Trust.* Since the abuser is most often a loved and trusted person in the child's life, a deep sense of betrayed trust pervades the child's view of life. Poor basic trust is a commonly observed characteristic of survivors.

2. *Interruption of Sexual Development.* This disruption of crucial psychological and sexual development naturally affects relationships. Anna Freud explains, "The abused young child . . . is not merely exposed to an unfortunate and unsuitable sexual encounter, he is also experiencing a type of stimulation for which, developmentally, he is wholly unprepared. . . . He is forced into premature phallic or genital development while his legitimate developmental needs and their accompanying mental expressions are bypassed."[1]

3. *Confusion of Roles.* In many cases of intrafamilial child sexual abuse, the child is forced into a premature adult role as lover-wife-partner. Caregivers on whom the child has every right to depend exploit the child's vulnerability and relate to the child in roles that are confusing and/or terrifying to the child.

4. *Loss of Childhood.* The abused child loses the experience and the memory of presexual personhood. Thrust into a world of emotional complexity, she has no opportunity to develop resources for dealing with adult life. Many survivors have lost not only those years of innocence but even the memory of

childhood. A blocking out of painful memories resulting in memory blanks is common among abuse survivors.

In Figure 3.1 we have summarized some of the problems experienced by survivors and their possible roots in the personal history of the survivor.

Variables in Degree of Damage

Why are some survivors able to cope fairly well with life while others spend their lives under psychiatric care? Naturally, there are many variables.

1. There appears to be a significant correlation between intensity of trauma and (a) the age difference between the partners and (b) the amount of coercion involved.[2]

2. There is evidence that sexual involvement with a family member is more disturbing than sexual experience with an unknown adult.[3] In fact, Allender asserts that, in general, damage will be most severe to the degree that the parental bond with the child is disturbed. The greater the failure of the parents to protect and care for the child, the harder will be her battle to trust others and to trust God.[4]

3. There is evidence that the degree of trauma increases with the duration of the abuse.[5]

Roots of Pain

A summary of some of the long-term effects experienced by survivors of child sexual abuse.

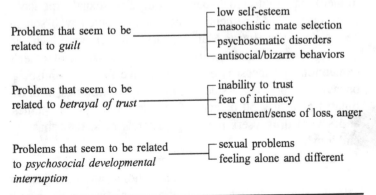

| Problems that seem to be related to *guilt* | low self-esteem
masochistic mate selection
psychosomatic disorders
antisocial/bizarre behaviors |

| Problems that seem to be related to *betrayal of trust* | inability to trust
fear of intimacy
resentment/sense of loss, anger |

| Problems that seem to be related to *psychosocial developmental interruption* | sexual problems
feeling alone and different |

Figure 3.1

4. The response of caregivers to a child's revelation of incest or abuse affects the long-term impact of the experience. Helen Hewitt, director of a Sexual Assault Center, tells us that there are two factors that may help minimize the damage to the child: the support of the non-offending parent offered to the child, and a confession and verbal assumption of responsibility by the offending party.

Steele and Alexander point out: "Some researchers seem to consider a person who is married and shows no serious psychotic, neurotic, or character disorder and who is living with average success within the community to have emerged from the sexual abuse unscathed. But . . . much pain and turmoil can exist beneath an outwardly normal or seemingly well-adjusted appearance."[6]

Most of the stories and voices we quote speak out of this hidden pain.

Behavioral Problems Resulting from Child Sexual Abuse

Many victims of child sexual abuse respond by negative and self-destructive behavior patterns. They may seek escape through substance abuse (alcohol or drug addiction). Many finally run away from home, an escape route that often ends in prostitution. Judianne Densen-Gerber's rehabilitative work in 1977 with young female drug abusers in seven states brought to the attention of the public the little-known fact (until then) that child sexual abuse was the first sexual experience of as many as 44 percent of the young women who sought help at Odyssey House. Many of these women were involved in prostitution as well as drug abuse. It is Densen-Gerber's contention that incest is often a causative factor in antisocial behavior.[7] More recent studies support these findings, with estimates of nearly 50 percent of female runaways, prostitutes, and severe drug users reporting histories of sexual abuse as children.[8]

Early sexual experiences often produce sexually precocious adolescents. Promiscuity is characteristic. It may be a form of self-punishment inflicted in an attempt to deal with the guilt experienced by victims. It may be a demonstration of low self-esteem or a form of further self-degradation. Or it may be a "repetition compulsion" in which, paradoxically, the teenager seeks to relieve the pain of the experiences by repeating them. This seems to be the opposite of what is expected as a response to negative experience, but these researchers suggest that by repetition, the young person attempts to achieve a measure of control over the experience, to work through attendant anxiety, and/or to find some replacement for the lost parent.[9]

Whatever the dynamics of promiscuity may be, teenage promiscuity is usually a cry for love and affection. Since the sexually abused girl confuses love, guilt, and sex, too often she ends up being used as a sexual object.[10] Teenagers who have received confusing signals from trusted adults about the way in which acceptance and love are expressed lack the ability to distinguish between genuine caring and casual sex.

Of course, various forms of "acting out," often including drug abuse, may be the child's way of finally getting even with parents who failed to give her the kind of care she needed.

Obviously, behavior aberrations such as substance abuse, general rebelliousness, and promiscuity complicate the problems of low self-esteem, guilt, and a general sense of lack of control over life and destiny. By the time some adult survivors are trying to put the pieces of the puzzle of life into some kind of meaningful arrangement, the pieces are often not only jumbled but also scarred and twisted.

Relationship Problems

The distorted relationships of a childhood marred by abuse also cast their long shadow across adult relationships in many areas.

1. *Marriage.* The betrayal of trust during childhood often makes it difficult for survivors to trust a man sufficiently to enter into a truly intimate marriage. Ambivalent feelings about sex, running the whole range from aversion to addiction, often lead to problems in sexual adjustment within marriage. What is clinically called "sexual dysfunction" may be experienced as lack of interest or disgust, a feeling of "deadness," flash-

backs of the abuse during sex, or compulsive behaviors such as masturbation or sexual addiction.[11]

Sexual problems may include vaginismus, a condition in which muscles near the vaginal opening contract involuntarily, making penetration painfully difficult or impossible. Flashback memories may be triggered during intercourse. (As one woman put it, "Suddenly, it wouldn't be my husband but my father.") Such waves of repugnant memories often cloud the marital sexual relationship with conflict and pain.

Since fully realized sexual communion is an extension of intimacy, the poor basic trust of many abuse survivors interferes with the development of mutually enjoyable marriage.

> *I seldom enjoy sex. I always wonder, "Does he love me or need me?"*

> *I cannot fully enjoy sexual intimacy with my husband—in fact, I'm really turned off. I do have intercourse with him, but it's more out of duty.*

> *My husband tells me he doesn't blame me, but somehow I'm never sure that I can believe him.*

> *I have a hard time believing anyone could really love me. I think my husband is tired of trying to convince me that he does.*

The anger the abused person has felt—and may continue to feel—toward the abuser may be generalized into a hostility against all men. Repressed anger may express itself in sudden outbursts of irrational anger.

> *I've had angry outbursts all through our marriage and felt used by my husband, without knowing why. Only recently, through therapy, have I begun to remember previously blocked memories of being fondled by my father.*

Many women are fearful of revealing their past to their husbands, some keeping their painful secret for many years before marital difficulties force them to seek counsel and frequently to share their whole story with their husbands.

> *I was afraid to tell my husband about my incestuous past for fear he would reject me. After therapy, when I finally told him, I kept waiting for him to say, "Why didn't you stop it?" but he never did. He never thought it was my fault.*

> *I was finally able to talk about the past and even in sessions with my husband to relate to him my experience. My husband was wonderful, and together we worked out this problem.*

> *We had been married a dozen years before I had the courage to tell my husband. He never said a word; he just took me in his arms and very tenderly made love to me.*

Clearly, many survivors are married to caring—if often puzzled—husbands. But others face another range of marriage problems. Many abuse survivors marry abusive, domineering, untrustworthy men, thus perpetuating the abuse cycle in their own lives and often in the lives of their daughters. Low self-esteem is a factor in making poor partnership choices.

> *I thought that all I could deserve was a nerd—so I married one.*

> *I couldn't believe that, with my past, I could deserve to have a Christian husband and a happy home.*

The "repetition compulsion" described earlier may also dictate the choice of an abusive husband. Or, to a survivor of child sexual abuse, an untrustworthy or uncommitted man may seem a less dangerous choice for a partner. She is scared of being disappointed again, and he will not raise her hopes too high. She is scared of losing control, and he will be easier to control than a man who is capable of true relationship. Further, his mistreatment of her serves as evidence for her self-perceived unworth.[12]

Whatever causes it, this pattern of choosing unworthy men to love has been noted as a frequently recurring pattern in the lives of many incest and abuse survivors. Meiselman notes, "the women . . . were not usually perceived as actively inviting abuse, but their willingness to tolerate mistreatment allowed them to endure relationships that a more mature, assertive woman would have ended or never begun at all."[13] In *The Broken Taboo*, Justice and Justice write:

> Sometimes . . . daughters from incestuous families will pick husbands who are indeed untrustworthy, immature, and unreliable. It is as if these are the only kind of men to whom they know how to relate. In a sense, the daughters . . . create a self-fulfilling prophecy. They expect to find men untrustworthy and they marry men who are just that.[14]

The women who have shared their stories with us are quite frank about this repeating cycle of abuse:

> *My first husband was a homosexual, and my second was physically violent with me for many years before I left him.*

> *I was sexually and physically abused in my adolescent years. . . . Then I was physically, emotionally, and mentally abused by my husband. I'm now divorced, trying to live a peaceful life.*

> *It seems as though I wear a sign around my neck that says, "Go ahead. Victimize me."*

Women who have been victimized as children and have learned passivity as a response are typically what researchers call *incest carriers*. That is, they marry the kind of men who abuse wives and children, and in their inability to defend themselves and/or their children, create a setting for such abuse that becomes a repeating cycle.

While problems in marriage relationships may loom larger than other relationship problems, it is a fact that sexually abused children often experience difficulty in any and all relationships. Many are mistrustful of people in general—and men in particular. Anger and hostility originally felt toward the abuser is generalized in a "chip on the shoulder" attitude toward everyone they know.

A lack of self-worth may mean that the abuse survivor has an excessive need for affirmation from others. And while she may crave affirmation, she may also discount any offered words of encouragement or praise. ("Oh, really? He's just saying that.") Words flung at a child during the growing-up years—"You're a no-good, just like your daddy," or, "If people knew what you were like, they wouldn't have anything to do with you"—continue to haunt the adult survivor. Badgered by self-doubt, she may be unable to believe that people really like her.

2. *Lesbianism.* For some abused women, the strong mistrust of men may lead toward lesbianism. A relationship with another woman may feel like a safer kind of sexual attachment. This link between child sexual abuse and homosexual practice has not been adequately understood or researched, but many women told us of homosexual experiences in their search for love. Meiselman found that seven of the twenty-three daughters in her sample who had experienced incest had "become gay or had significant experiences or conflicts centered on homosexual feelings."[15]

3. *Parenting.* In parenting, the abuse survivor may have to fight two opposing tendencies: repeating abusive patterns of behavior, and reacting by overprotectiveness. We learn parenting from our parents. The abuse survivor works from poor models and is often unsure of herself. In addition, she may be mistrustful of all adults who relate to her children, or even

openly suspicious of her husband as he relates to their daughters.

And, of course, survivors have difficult relationships with the parents who failed to give them the kind of care they needed as children. Many are torn by conflicting emotions toward their parents—feeling both love and hatred, both forgiveness and anger.

"Flayed to the core of my spirit" is how one woman described herself. Many survivors will identify with her. For most people, relationships are at the very center of life. Many survivors respond to their difficulties in destructive ways. Depression may deepen to suicidal intensity. Living out what often seems to be a ruined life, many survivors struggle to find the strength to meet life on a day-to-day basis.

Certainly these women have earned the right to be heard. We stand in awe of their ability to survive, their tenacity in building and rebuilding their lives and relationships. The church must listen and respond as a family to abuse survivors.

The Church Can Help
For survivors, the greatest need is to be accepted, loved, and affirmed as persons of worth. The church is uniquely endowed by the Spirit of God to become this place of acceptance. To be received and loved as a person is the beginning of wholeness.

According to Heggen, the most important action a congregation can take in supporting and healing survivors of child sexual abuse is to smash the silence, secrecy, and denial around the topic of sexual abuse.

> How can victims be expected to share their stories of abuse with people who haven't even acknowledged the existence of such a problem among them? When sexual abuse is named in the church, victims may come to see the church as a likely and appropriate place to go for support in their painful journeys toward healing.[16]

Once the church begins to recognize its responsibility and grace-granted ability to offer affection apart from sex, to meet the need of abuse survivors "to be affirmed as individuals independent of their sexuality,"[17] it will also, we hope, find its voice. For the church must not only listen to but also speak for these courageous survivors.

4
The Shadowed Spirit

Kathy's Story

During my teen years, I did go to church quite regularly. I had found an evangelical church near our new home, and—all on my own, since my parents weren't interested in "religion" at all—I began attending. I heard the gospel explained clearly as I became a part of the Sunday school and youth program. I gave full intellectual assent to the truth that God, in his great love for me, had sent his Son, Jesus Christ, to die for my sins. I believed, too, that Jesus rose again from the dead and that he could offer eternal life to those who would come to him.

I responded with an invitation to Jesus to come into my life, making a sort of initial commitment of my life to him. But that did not really affect my life. I was a very confused person. I was, for instance, sharply aware that my dating behavior did not tally with a Christian commitment. My past was completely undealt with.

When I did finally get some psychiatric help after my suicide attempt, the psychiatrist blamed the church for making me feel guilty. Instead of helping me face my guilt, he suggested that since the church made me feel guilty, I should stop attending. (I have to make some allowance for the doctor; I had withheld the most important facts from him, so his assessment and treatment were limited and ineffective.)

I took his advice and stopped going to church. Yet although I drifted far from my spiritual moorings, I somehow knew that the answer lay, finally, with God. Meanwhile, my confused and miserable life went on.

———————

Like Kathy, many survivors of sexual abuse have intense spiritual conflicts which may be little understood by those who have not experienced their pain. It is not surprising that something as traumatic and disruptive as child sexual abuse should have implications for spiritual life and growth. We are not merely "spirits within a body," but persons integrated in such a way that what affects the body also affects the spirit.

The spiritual dimension of recovery from child sexual abuse has just recently begun to be explored by research.[1] The voices in our sample spoke out clearly from *within* the church. These people identified a number of specific areas of spiritual struggle that they relate to their experiences of molestation.

> *Help! Sometimes I think my life is over and have thoughts of suicide. I'm a believer but feel that even God hates me and without him there's no meaning to life.*

———————

> *I don't feel God really loves me—and I've been willing to accept that because I haven't felt that I deserved his love.*

———————

> *When I was young, I was abused by my stepfather. It has short-circuited all my attempts at a relationship with God.*

Sadly, the church has, as a whole, shown very little comprehension of the problems faced by sexual abuse survivors. A quick prayer, a pat Scripture text, and we expect that deeply wounded people will somehow be healed.

> *My Christian friend tells me I should be more up than*

*down if I truly love Jesus as my Savior. She comes across
as very condemning of me.*

Charles Colson speaks of this attitude in his essay, "On Christianity and Magic Wands":

> Much of today's teaching and preaching communicates
> Christianity as an instant fix to all of our pains and struggles. Consequently, we begin to think of our faith as a
> sparkling magic wand: we wave it, and presto, our problems are gone in a puff of smoke. . . . This is, bluntly
> put, heresy. . . . It not only makes Christians incredibly
> naive in approaching complex problems, but it can shatter the fragile faith of the believer who expects the magic
> wand to work every time. When those problems don't
> disappear . . . he questions whether his spirituality is
> faulty. The result is guilt. . . . If we trust this fairy-tale
> brand of Christianity, we eventually fall victim to its consequent paralysis . . . as we confront our own repeated
> sins and failures, [and] as we encounter the stumblings
> of those to whom we minister.[2]

The simplistic idea communicated in the church that "Jesus is
the answer" may often be begging the question. Of course we
believe and affirm Jesus to be the answer—but not in any
easy, superficial way, built on repressing memories and pasting
on false smiles. We believe in the deep work of his healing,
resurrection life.

Learning to Trust

Survivors of abusive childhoods have some especially difficult
problems with coming to faith as well as with living a faith-filled life. We have already commented on the deficiency of
basic trust that characterizes many survivors. Obviously, this
impaired ability to trust anyone interferes with a person's ability
to become a Christian. If it is hard to trust other people, it can
be hard to trust God as well. In a study of adult Christian women
who were sexually abused as children, Terese A. Hall found that
the early abuse significantly affected these women's trust that

God loves and will take care of them.[3] Heggen writes:

> Profound spiritual damage occurs . . . when the abuser
> and victim are religious people. If the victim called out
> to God for protection during her time of abuse, yet the
> abuse continued, she may subsequently view God as un-
> caring. She may see God as aloof, disinterested in both
> the human condition and her personal well-being, impo-
> tent to intervene in human matters.[4]

When trust is affirmed again and again during the growing-up
years, a person may at times recognize and have to deal with
fears that crop up like occasional weeds in a field of flowers.
But for a person who has had her trust betrayed consistently,
a general attitude of fearfulness develops, with only an occasional bloom of faith in the weed-filled garden of the spirit.
In our lives, however, we grow what we cultivate, and even
a tiny, mustard seed-sized bit of faith can grow into a life-
changing belief in God and his goodness. For the abuse
survivor, the process of making an emotional commitment
to God and nurturing that faith may be a long and demanding concern.

Then, too, a relationship with God demands an open trans-
parency, an honesty about one's own personhood, which may
be difficult for abuse survivors. They are mask-wearers, hiding
behind carefully constructed facades. They are skilled at keeping relationships safely at an arm's length. Becoming vulnerable to anyone, God included, may cause great anxiety and
deep misgivings. When fathers and father figures have caused
the abuse, the problems with coming to Christian faith are
even greater.

I must have "received" Jesus literally hundreds of times,
but I never had any assurance that he had really come
into my life.

I was never able to see God as "Abba" or to have a
real understanding of God as Father. . . . I never let

*anyone into my place of safety because I felt I wasn't
worth it—and besides, I couldn't even trust God not to
hurt me.*

How tragic that fathers—some of them Christian—would do
the very thing that would deface the divine image for a child.

How can one learn to trust a Father God when an earthly
father has been an exploiter? It may not be easy, but as the
character of God emerges from Scripture study, new under-
standings begin to take hold. The steadfastness of God's love
is the theme of the writers of the Psalms; again and again they
celebrate it. God is the Holy Father to the fatherless and the
One who can heal the crippled faculty of faith in the torn
hearts of abuse survivors.

The loving embodiment of faithfulness in God's children
can help the survivors come to an understanding of the goodness of God. The loyalty of Christians as a surrogate family
can help to remodel family roles. The love of brothers and
sisters in Christ can rebuild shattered self-esteem. And a deepening understanding of the Scriptures can help the survivor
build a new life.

Overcoming Guilt and Guilt Feelings

The intense struggle with guilt and guilt feelings which most
abuse survivors experience has, of course, deep implications
for their spiritual lives.

*I still have trouble believing God can't see the things
I've done wrong and trouble understanding that
Christ's death erased the sins. They say it will come
in time.*

---

*I was molested by a baby sitter when I was three or
four; when I was nine I was raped by my brother and
sold to his friends. Hate for my brother grew along
with my lack of self-respect. I went to Bible College
still feeling unclean and unworthy of a Christian man
and home.*

We have already discussed some of the reasons for the over-whelming guilt experienced by most sexual abuse survivors. "Amid her craving for love, her seemingly voluntary involve-ment in the incest, her possible enjoyment of it, and her com-plicity in the cover-up, the victim comes away . . . with overwhelming feelings of responsibility and guilt."[5] And in chapter 6, we will talk in some detail about entering into a sense—as well as a state—of being fully forgiven.

For the abuse survivor who desires to enter into a full Chris-tian experience, the issue is a crucial one. Francis Schaeffer's words about guilt are particularly applicable to survivors with guilt confusion:

> There is a danger that the orthodox Christian will fail to realize that at times guilt-feelings are present when no true guilt exists. Let us remember that the Fall resulted in division not only between God and man, and man and man, but between man and himself. Hence there are psy-chological guilt-feelings without true guilt. In such cases we must show genuine compassion.[6]

Of course, for the adult survivor, as with any human being, there will be sin that needs to be confessed and turned away from. We have all sinned. We all need forgiveness, cleansing, the chance to start anew.

The rough and careless hand of another may have spilled the ink that stains my carpet. But it is still my carpet. And it is still stained and in need of cleansing, like those who have been stained by sexual abuse. Fortunately, the words of Scrip-ture come with reassurance: "the blood of Jesus . . . purifies us from all sin" (1 John 1:7). The sacrifice Jesus made on the cross is sufficient to cleanse from all that defiles me: my own sin, the sin of another against me.

The ancient rite of absolution is the means by which the church traditionally has spoken the words of forgiveness guar-anteed by the death of Christ. Today the words of absolution may need to be spoken by a doctor, a counselor, a friend. Dr. John White, psychiatrist and author, tells of such a case. A severely depressed man had failed to respond to normal psychiatric treatment. White found that the man was troubled by things he remembered as sins.

"What about forgiveness?" I asked him.

"I want it so bad."

"What's your religion?"

"Russian Orthodox."

"And what does your priest say about how you get to be forgiven?"

"He doesn't talk too much. We go to confession."

"And what does that do?"

"I don't often go."

I groped for words. "But if you do go, why would God forgive you?"

"Because Christ died. He shed blood."

"So?"

"I'm too bad for that."

Unaccountably I grew angry. No logical reason. It just happened. "What do you mean you're too bad?"

His voice was rising like my own. "I don't deserve ever to be forgiven."

"You're darn right you don't! . . . Who do you think you are to say Christ's death was not enough for you? Who are you to feel you must add your miserable pit-

---

Something You Can Do Right Now

Here are some Scripture passages for you to read, meditate on, and think through, concerning the truth of God's forgiveness. As you make them your own through reading and re-reading, and perhaps through memorizing, you will come to know the truth of God's forgiveness even if you have no particular accompanying feeling just now. Joy will spring from the truth as you accept it and make it your own.

Scriptures about Forgiveness

1. Provision is made for our forgiveness in the atoning death of our Lord: 2 Corinthians 5:21; Isaiah 53; 1 Peter 2:24
2. Forgiveness is rooted in the faithfulness and justice of God: Romans 3:23-26; 1 John 1:8-10
3. A prayer for forgiveness: Psalm 51
4. A celebration of forgiveness: Psalm 32; Revelation 1:5-6

tance to the great gift God offers you? Is his sacrifice
not good enough?"

Dr. White reports that, at this point, realization dawned on the
man and he began to cry and pray at once: "God . . . I
didn't mean to offend you . . . God, thank you . . . It's amazing . . . I didn't know it worked like that . . . Thank you."[7]
And from that moment, the man moved toward health and
wholeness.

The person whose conscience has been stained needs to
enter into understanding about:

1. The responsibility of the adult initiator for the sexual
    abuse. (Karin Meiselman says, "Nothing that a child
    does justifies sexual approaches from a parent."[8])
2. The reality of one's own sinfulness.
3. The incredible power of Christ's sacrifice to atone for
    sin and "cleanse our consciences from acts that lead
    to death, so that we may serve the living God!" (He-
    brews 9:14).

For some, there may be a strong emotional accompaniment
to forgiveness: a feeling of release, or, as Kathy describes it,
"a cool, clean breeze blowing through me." For others, there
may be no particular feeling. God's forgiveness is a fact to
be received by faith. It is an objective truth that "if we confess

---

Prayer of Forgiveness
You may want to write out your act of forgiveness, either in this book or
on a piece of paper, or in a journal. Be very specific. Write:
Lord, I have sinned. This is the name of my sin: _____
_____. I am truly sorry. Please forgive me and make
me clean. Help me to hear in my heart those words you spoke so often,
"My child, _____, your sins are forgiven you." Amen.
    Lord, this person has sinned against me. I forgive _____
for _____. I am willing to take the pain. In
my mind's eye, I am going to stand at the foot of the cross and hear
you say, "Forgive him, for he knows not what he did." I am going to
bring my pain and place it before you. I bring it to you; now take it
from me, and release me from its weight. Amen.

our sins, he is faithful and just and will forgive us our sins"
(1 John 1:9). God's forgiveness is rooted in *who he is* and in
the *provision made for us in Jesus' death on our behalf.* It
does not depend on how we feel.

This is particularly important to grasp when the whole emotional self has been wounded by abuse. The abuse survivor
has to look beyond herself to find reference points. We suggest
again that the Bible provides such reference points—stars to
steer by even when any sense of direction is otherwise lost.

Difficulty in Receiving Love Messages

The low self-esteem that characterizes many survivors of
abuse often interferes with receiving love messages from other
people as well as from God.

> *I was molested at nine years of age and still, more than
> fifty years later, I live under the burden of this awful
> abuse, feeling dirty and unfit before God.*

> *I figured at one time that God couldn't love me and that
> I was going to go to hell no matter what I did, so it
> didn't matter if I lived or died.*

Dr. Heggen finds that many child sexual abuse survivors feel
that God has abandoned them. Some blame God for the abuse
while others blame themselves. If God let the abuse happen,
they reason, it must have been because they deserved it. Either
God did not love them or they are unworthy of divine love.
Either way, these thoughts cause survivors to struggle in trying
to accept God's love.[9]

In an earlier chapter we talked about the survivor's need
for excessive reassurance. It is this same need for more-than-
reasonable reassurance and reinforcement that interferes with
confidence in one's spiritual life. Fortunately, the promises and
assurances of God are written—and can be read as many times
as needed until the truth washes through the mind and reaches
the shadowed spirit. We have often suggested that key Scriptures be written out on note cards and placed on mirrors, re-

frigerator doors, cupboards—wherever they are accessible for frequent re-reading, memorizing, and meditation.

Lack of Understanding and Compassion within the Church

As we have noted, survivors of abuse have often found little acceptance and support within the Christian community.

> *The abused most often turn away from God; and when we have sought God, often we are further abused emotionally by the children of God. The church does not understand our pain.*

> *It has been a struggle finding answers to the effects of the abuse I suffered in my home. The church seemed only concerned with its "name" and did not try to help me when I needed and approached it.*

> *People in churches today don't want to know about abuse. They seem to feel it is the victim's fault.*

> *I did have one counseling session with my pastor, but it seems he thinks this should have healed me.*

It is ironic that the church, which should represent the compassion and the power of Jesus Christ in the lives of wounded,

---

Something You Can Do Right Now

1. Look up Romans 5:1-11. Put your name in appropriate places in these verses. The truth that comes through the Scriptures is that God's love is extended to us as we are. And so there is hope.

2. Practice accepting the loving, encouraging words from others, instead of deflecting them. You will find that gradually the darkened rooms of your spirit will open to the warm sunlight of love as expressed in God's Word and world, and as modeled in at least some of the people in your life.

brokenhearted people, has so sadly failed to listen and respond. There is little doubt in our minds that the long-time male domination of the church has left it crippled in ministering to women who have been hurt by men. But we are beginning to listen, beginning to hear. The voices are coming through. And by encouraging, comforting, and journeying with the abused as friends, we can help each other press on.

5
Claiming the Past

Kathy's Story

After our daughter was born, we moved to another area, and I thought, *Oh, good. A fresh start. I won't have to drive by that store where I shoplifted. I'll never have to see that court-house again.* It was like I was going into a new world, and things would be different. You kid yourself into thinking a new environment will make the old one go away.

But I soon found that my problems had moved with me. I had a fourth child, and when he was about three months old I found myself again in terrible depression. The old suicidal feelings were overwhelming. One day, in desperation, I phoned a minister from a local church. I didn't know him and he didn't know me. But he came, and for the first time I told my story. The whole story.

I'm sure it was good for me to finally say it. But once I had told him, he didn't seem to know what to do for me. He just said a quick prayer and left.

As he went out my front door, I ran up the stairs, crying. I got down by my bed on my knees, crying out, "God, I don't know if you are real. I don't know if you are there. But if you are real, you are going to have to do something because I don't know what to do. I don't know where to turn."

After I had prayed and cried and become silent, I became

very clearly conscious of a single phrase: "Be still and know that I am God."

I didn't even know that this was a line of Scripture. I just grasped those words like a lifeline. I lived on those words for a whole year. When flashbacks flooded over me, I said them. I quoted them when anger rose like an animal inside me, raging for release. "Be still. Be still and know that I am God." After doing this many times a day for several days, I began to realize that something was changing. The spaces between flashbacks were getting longer, and one day I realized with joy, *It's been two or three days*.

And then a friend invited me to a women's Bible study. At first, I didn't go regularly, just once in a while. They provided baby-sitting, and if for no other reason, it was worth my while to have someone look after my four kids for a morning. A few months later, my friend invited me to go with her to a Christian conference. I really didn't want to go. I didn't think I could stand a whole day of religion. But I ended up going.

As we continue to follow Kathy's story, we note that she has now taken a very significant step. She has told somebody about her past, and by verbalizing it she has claimed it as her own.

Every one of us is a sum total of past experiences and perceptions. When we cut ourselves off from our pasts, we cut ourselves off from our own identities. We are less than whole. The whole and healthy person embraces both past and future.

But for abuse survivors with their pain-filled and blighted childhood memories, a lot of courage is needed, and often the help of a counselor or therapist, for them to be able to say, "This is what happened to me. This is also a part of my life. This, too, I will claim as part of my story." Many abuse survivors have repressed distressing memories so completely and for so long that there are large memory gaps in their personal histories.

I am a recovering alcoholic. I was sexually molested by my father and oldest brother from the time I was eight until I was fourteen. The molestation only came out in therapy. I had subconsciously blocked it out—and it is causing a lot of pain and depression for me.

I was sexually and physically abused as a child, and God is helping me remember more about the abuse, thus creating healing after thirty years of blocking out that anything happened to me.

I kept the secret of my childhood molestation within me until I was in late mid-life. I suffered torment all those years—had a nervous breakdown in my thirties and even attempted suicide in my early fifties. I have now told my family and feel released after many years of suffering.

My first sexual experience was at age four. I just spent the last year and a half in therapy. It was a real struggle to face the truth. A part of me didn't want to accept it.

I, too, am a victim of sexual abuse. It has only been in the last three years that I was able to talk about it. I had kept it hidden inside me for over twenty years. Even though I thought I had "gotten over it," and no one else knew about it, the scars were there and it finally had to come out.

If you are an abuse survivor, an important first step toward your healing is to put words to your past, to verbalize it to another person. A young woman who leads an Incest Survivors Group urges, "It's very important to be able to tell what happened to you, to talk about it in any kind of language you want to use. It's a way of saying, 'Yes, it did happen. But it's not my whole story.' "

Paying Attention to Painful Memories

The subconscious mind can be compared to a large house with many rooms. When pain from the past is locked away and not dealt with, some closets or rooms are sealed and are no longer available to us as spaces for living, for loving. Reclaiming our pasts means opening up all those closed places in our lives. Fortunately, God has given us a "tidy housekeeper," a natural cleansing agent within our subconscious that tries to draw our attention to the boarded-up places of our lives.

Here are some of the ways in which our attention may be drawn to problems by our subconscious.

1. *Dreams.* Recurring dreams, especially those that have repetitive symbolic patterns accompanied by emotionally weighted significance, may be an eruption into the conscious mind of concerns buried deeply in the subconscious. In *Daddy's Girl,* Charlotte Vale Allen tells of a nightmare that continued to haunt her long into adult life, a nightmare in which she is threatened by a man with a knife.[1]

The phallic symbolism, the emotional terrorism, of that dream is pretty obvious. Through dreams, the subconscious mind may be issuing an order: "Pay attention. There is something I am trying to remind you of, something locked away that is not yet resolved."

2. *Erratic behavior.* Inexplicable rage, such as the anger Kathy describes as "an animal inside me, raging for release," is something that many abuse survivors experience. When anger seems to explode out of proportion to the incident that triggered it, one needs to ask whether its true source is hidden away in the inaccessible regions of the memory.

Sudden feelings of self-hatred or unreasonable intolerance are other clues to buried problems. (One woman told me of having an overwhelming aversion to a son-in-law who reminded her of her childhood abuser. Once she realized why she felt that way toward the inoffensive young man her daughter had married, she was able to deal with her feelings about him.) Kathy's wild driving and shoplifting are examples of bizarre behavior triggered by subconscious factors—but remarkably typical in stories told by abuse survivors.

3. *Physical illness or psychosomatic pain.* When the mind is troubled by painful memories, the body may well suffer—as Shakespeare showed us so memorably in the illness of Lady MacBeth. When we experience illness for which there is no apparent physical explanation, we should listen for the signals that are coming to us of wounds that need to be healed, of memories that may be haunting us because they have never been allowed to surface and be dealt with.

If we understand how the subconscious works to try to help us deal with long-buried problems, we should feel no embarrassment at discovering a psychosomatic illness. Instead of feeling apologetic, we should heed the signal, even respond with, "If this is a clue, if this pain (this headache, stomach cramp, burning, dizziness) is an indicator of some deep turmoil within me, how fortunate I am! What kind of intriguing possibilities of self-knowledge lie ahead?"

But Do I Have to Talk about It?

"It all happened so long ago," one woman commented. "I don't even want to think about it, let alone talk about it. Why do I have to talk about it now?" There are a number of reasons why speaking of the past is helpful and may well be a first step toward healing. As we discussed in the first part of this chapter, it helps to accept your own past as a fact—you were abused as a child. It must be acknowledged. Second, there is a catharsis, or purging, of painful memories in the telling. In a book called *Carol's Story,* author Chip Ricks recorded the pain-filled life story of a sexually abused girl. Carol says:

> Having suffered from the deep wounds of child abuse . . . I realize that my story must be told not only for the others' sake but for my own, as part of the healing process that God, the Great Physician, has for me. . . . I have always sensed at moments of crisis in my life that I had to face the truth and tell it in its entirety, no matter how painful the process. I know that only the truth, bitter as it is, can make me whole and set me free.[2]

This is not to suggest that a survivor should talk to just anyone about the past. A close friend can be a listener, but it is probably wisest to choose someone who can be trusted with a secret. For some, a trained counselor or therapist will be the best choice—and we'll look at how to choose and find such a person in a later chapter.

> *I did find an excellent Christian counselor. . . . Bringing the abuse to the front where I could face it was the difficult part. I do want to explore my past, but oh, it hurts so much!*

> *I admire those who can talk about it. I still cry when I talk about the sexual abuse in my life.*

> *The last two years of my life have been very hard because of my childhood story of abuse. I suppressed it for thirty-eight years, and now I feel like I opened something terrible—it overwhelms me.*

Many women wonder how to go about telling their husbands. Again, the real questions you should ask are: Can he handle this information? Will it improve or work against your relationship? Since openness and honesty are necessary to the full development of mutuality in marriage, you—like most wives—will probably want to share your story with your husband. However, the best place to do this may be in a counselor's office, with a third party to help in creating a setting for you to share your story, and also to help your husband deal with his own grief and anger.

You may not feel that you know someone in whom to confide just now. But whether you do or not, writing in a journal is often helpful, serving as a way of verbalizing your past and getting it into perspective. Writing things down has a way of getting them out into the open, into the sunlight. Writing in a journal might help you prepare for sharing your story with another person—a sort of rehearsal (see the "Something You Can Do Right Now" exercise on the next page).

*Eighteen months ago I found Jesus as my own personal
Savior. (I should say that he found me!) The first thing
I learned is how to journal. I am beginning to understand
some things. But whereas for some people everything
happens quickly, for me it has been a slow deepening,
learning, loving, and doing process.*

What about the Anger?

*In my heart I want to fly, but I have these things that
weigh me down. The Lord and I work on them as I can
handle the knowledge, and he helps me control the rage
inside of me. He knows my expanse for rage—but really
my true desire is to love people.*

Most of the women who speak from the experience of abuse
speak of the anger that burns deep within them, anger that
often erupts uninvited and is often vented on undeserving targets: husbands, children, neighbors—often just about anyone
within range can become the "whipping post."

There's not a doubt in the world about this: Anger is a
highly appropriate emotion as a consequence of child sexual
abuse. *Of course you feel angry*—and so do those of us who
have listened to your stories. We personally feel such deep
anger at the thought of children whose trust is betrayed, whose

---

Something You Can Do Right Now

Choose a notebook you can call your own. Put today's date at the top of
that first clean page. Here are some ideas to help you get started.

1. You can write your journal as "The Book of My Life." You'll find
   helpful suggestions for chapter headings in Ron Klug's *How to Keep
   a Spiritual Journal* in the chapter titled "Looking Backward."[3]

2. You may choose to write your journal in the form of personal letters.
   You can address your letters to

   —yourself as a child

   —your own children

   —your mother or father

   —your abuser

   —God

(It's not likely that you'll actually mail the letters to any of the above, but
it is helpful for you to have the sense that you are writing to somebody.)

innocence is plundered, that we often pray, "Oh, God! Defender of the defenseless, father to the fatherless, arise and judge those who hurt these little ones."

So it's not the anger itself that is wrong. In *Anger: The Misunderstood Emotion,* Carol Tavris points out that anger is a powerful motivator to move us to change things that are wrong. "Rage, I believe, is essential to the first phase of social movement."[4] Such a rage is being felt right now as our society becomes aroused against the selfish exploitation of children. Tavris points out, "Anger, like love, is a moral emotion. I have watched people use anger . . . to erode affection and trust, whittle away their spirits in bitterness and revenge, diminish their dignity. . . . And I watch with admiration those who use anger to probe for truth, who challenge the complacent injustices of life."[5]

To those who are angry because of their abuse experiences, we would like to suggest this: Embrace the anger. Do not deny it. "Press against the pain," and dare to call evil that which *is* evil. It is anger denied, repressed, misdirected, that does so much damage to ourselves and to others. Pushed down into our subconscious minds, anger is often what causes deep depression and uncontrolled outbursts.

There is nothing wrong with feeling angry at your violator. Nor is it wrong to feel angry with God. A young woman told us, "If I had told to tell people in my church what happened to me, they would probably have died of shock. Then somebody would have said, 'God can help you,' and I would have said, 'Well, he hasn't yet.' I can remember lying in my bed for hours praying, 'God, please stop this'—and blaming God for what was happening to me."

Why wouldn't a little child cry out, "Oh, God, where were you when I needed you? Why did you let this happen?" The good news is that God is great enough to bear our anger. He can absorb its full impact. It is safe to spend our anger against his bosom until, in the quiet, he lets us feel the pulse of his own broken heart.

Pastoral counselor Frank Lake writes:

The cross of Christ is intended to draw upon himself the

righteous anger of the innocent afflicted, who could not defend themselves or retaliate sufficiently to halt the injustice at the time and who tend therefore to delay and inevitably to displace the reaction, so that other relatively or totally innocent people suffer. Christ was crucified in order that now our anger can spend itself, obediently and in faith, hurting the one provided, the Lamb of God.[6]

Once you realize that anger is legitimate—and even healthy—once you turn it *upward,* instead of outward toward others or inward onto yourself, you will find yourself freed from its control.

Getting a Grip on Your Future

What I gained from our Incest Survivors Group was this: a sense of hope, the feeling that change is within my power.

One of the most liberating things you can learn is that while your past may have been under the domination of someone else, the future is yours. You cannot change the past or erase it, but you can determine, with God's help, to prevent it from controlling your future.

One woman related that she was learning to pray a prayer that embraced all of her life. It went like this:

For all that is behind, thanks.
For all that is ahead, yes.

For many abuse survivors, to pray such a prayer is like grasping a bouquet of roses firmly by the thorny stems. How can you be thankful for a childhood that has been marred and scarred by another's evil? The only way is to become thankful for who you are. Here's what one survivor says about it: "I thank God even for the painful things in my life because I have learned from them." And Kathy, our storyteller, could finally say, "I can at last truly say that I am not sorry that it happened to me. God is working out his purposes through the pain, and I thank him."

We stand in awe of such women who have been transformed by the grace of God into persons of great dignity and beauty. They have had the courage to look into their personal nights, to claim their own painful pasts. And in the daring to trust God for a different kind of future, they have found not only healing but also the glad hope of new beginnings.

6
The Freedom of Forgiveness

Kathy's Story

The all-day conference I attended with my friend was the turning point in my life. The speaker was Karen Mains, and the topic was forgiveness.

As she talked about how our subconscious minds deal with guilt, I suddenly felt as though she were describing me—from the inside out. She explained that our subconscious mind suppresses guilt, pushing it down until finally it surfaces in various ways: in erratic behavior, in anger, in depression. I knew all too well everything she was describing.

At the end of the session, Karen had everybody close their eyes, and then she began talking quietly to those of us who had been hurt by other people. "You may be here today carrying the wounds of another person's sin against you," she said. And then she explained that there were two kinds of guilt: guilt that other people put on us by hurting us and sinning against us, and guilt caused by things we have done ourselves. And I was experiencing both kinds of guilt. Guilt upon guilt.

"If you are experiencing guilt of your own, ask God to forgive you," Karen said.

That was not hard for me. I was sitting there saying, "Yes,

Lord, I have a lot of guilt. I ask you to forgive me now." And I sensed that he did forgive me.

Then Karen went on. "Now, if someone else has hurt you, I want you to ask God for strength to forgive that person."

I just sat there, stunned. I couldn't believe what she was saying. I thought, *She can't mean this. She can't be asking me to forgive my uncle.* She kept talking about giving our past with all of its pain to Jesus, and asking him to help us forgive that individual who had hurt us.

I sat there in my seat, and in my mind I said, *No way. He doesn't deserve to be forgiven. There's no way I'm going to let him off the hook. I can't forgive him, and I won't forgive him.*

And then I realized what I was saying. Here I was, just having asked God to forgive me, but I wasn't willing to extend forgiveness, to offer my uncle what I had just asked for myself.

And Karen kept saying, "Now forgive . . . forgive . . ."

My fists were clenched and I was actually gritting my teeth. I was desperately torn. But finally, reluctantly, needing God's forgiveness too much myself to hold onto this pain, I said, *O.K., then. Lord, I'm willing to forgive him.*

It was a most reluctant obedience, but God honored it. It was as much as I was able to do at the time. I'll never forget that second as long as I live. There I sat in a room with six or seven hundred other women, and I felt like I was alone with God. From the bottom of my feet up through my whole body a great weight simply disappeared.

The feeling was almost indescribable—like a cool, clean breeze blowing through me. And I knew that something had happened in that moment of forgiveness. I knew that I was never going to be the same. I never talked with anybody about it. I just quietly left the conference. But I went out of there knowing I was changed.

There had been a tremendous snowstorm that day, and it took us hours to get home. When I got there, my husband was shoveling the driveway. I said to him, "My life's never going to be the same from this day on. I don't know what has happened, and I can't explain it yet, but I'm sure things are going to be different."

The inward change was soon obvious. Love, joy, peace—the very things I had longed for but never known for more than a few minutes at a time—became real for me. My husband said to the kids, "I don't know what's happened to Mommy—but we have a new mommy in this house."

The flashbacks ceased immediately. The healing I am describing happened more than five years ago, and only twice in those five years have I ever again had a flashback. That abrupt change was inexplicable, because I had struggled with those memories all through the years. It was as though God erased a painful part of my memories.

At last I was able to tell my husband about my pain-filled childhood. He had no idea of it until about three months after my initial "freeing," when I told him about it. He was wonderful—he took it as information that would help him understand me better. What a relief to have him sharing my life fully! He had always been good to me; now my love and respect for him are simply limitless.

As for the guilt I had carried so long, there was a tremendous, immediate release. I thought then that this problem was dealt with forever. I didn't realize that there was deeper healing still to come.

At the moment Kathy realized she could be free of the hatred and resentment that held her prisoner, she also realized she had a choice to make. She could pick up the key that was offered, open her prison of pain, and walk out free. Or she could reject the idea. The key of forgiveness is, after all, a heavy one, and it is a painful struggle to turn it in rusty locks.

Kathy chose to take the heavy key and turn it in the locks of her soul, stiff and rusted as they were. And suddenly she was wonderfully free. Free to accept the forgiveness of God for her own sins; free from her abuser's death-clasp on her life.

Forgiveness Is a Choice

One of the hardest things for me to do is to forgive my father. I pray about it because I know forgiveness is im-

portant. The Lord has forgiven me, but it is very hard.

Forgiveness is a choice that each of us has the opportunity to make—not only once but many times throughout life. And each time we choose to forgive, we make a choice for freedom. Lewis Smedes says, "When you forgive someone who hurt you, you are dancing to the rhythm of the divine heartbeat, . . . you are in tune with the music of the universe. You are riding the crest of love, the energy of the cosmos."[1]

"I can't forgive my father," a young woman says through clenched teeth. "He ruined my life." The strange paradox of the whole matter is that until she forgives her father, he (although now in jail) has the power to go on ruining her life. When she makes the choice to forgive him, his power over her life is destroyed.

In *Great Expectations,* Charles Dickens creates an unforgettable metaphor for the damage caused in a life by the failure to forgive. Miss Havisham, jilted as a bride many years earlier, sits in her horrible, cobwebbed bridal chambers, wearing her yellowed wedding dress. She explains to Pip: "On this day of the year, long before you were born, this heap of decay . . . was brought here. It and I have worn away together. The mice have gnawed at it, and sharper teeth than teeth of mice have gnawed at me."[2] The destructive influence of her vindictive resentment in the lives of both Pip and Estella is a parable of the kind of damage that unforgiveness works. Men and women have testified that unforgiveness wreaks havoc again and again in the life of the person who harbors it, as well as in the lives of others.

The difficulty of forgiving—and the importance of it for reclaiming one's own life and for living in freedom from the control of the past—runs like a theme through the stories women have shared:

> *I am working with a counselor to deal with the intense emotion—mostly the anger, but also the guilt, shame, fear, pain, bitterness, and confusion I am feeling as a result of abuse. I have a problem with these negative emotions as a Christian. Christians shouldn't feel these*

emotions . . . forgive and forget and all that jazz.

I know I have to deal with what happened to me as a child instead of letting it lay in darkness in my heart and fester. I must forgive.

My parents are both dead, and I went to their graves to get rid of my feelings, and I found the anger and hate are still there. I wasn't ready to forgive him for what he had done to me.

For most of us, forgiving someone who has hurt us deeply is too hard to do without help. The choice we have to make is to be *willing to forgive.*

What Is Forgiveness?
Forgiving is not excusing. Though understanding some of the reasons for abuse is helpful, no one is asking you to say, "It's O.K.—he couldn't help himself." It's *not* O.K., and forgiveness operates in clear acknowledgment that we have been hurt, that we have been sinned against. In fact, forgiving can only happen in the light of a moral judgment.

When we offer forgiveness, we do several things.

1. *We transfer the case to a higher court.* When we forgive, we file a Quit Claim. We say, "I will no longer demand an accounting."

A good definition of forgiveness from Webster's Dictionary is "to give up all claim to punish or to exact penalty for an offense." As long as we are unforgiving, we hold the person who hurt us responsible to us. We demand an accounting. We may desire to get even, to injure the person in return for our injury. Many abuse survivors have told of harboring a desire to murder their abuser—and it's hard not to sympathize with that feeling. But it is destructive and life-threatening—not so much to the person who is hated with murderous intensity as to the person who hates and harbors the consuming desire for revenge.

In forgiving, we acknowledge the wrong done to us but commit that person to a higher Judge. We say in forgiving, "I am letting go of my desire to punish that person. I am turning him over to God." (It is something like stopping being a vigilante and turning the offender over to established justice.)

2. *We let go of our resentment.* A second aspect of forgiveness is to "give up resentment . . . stop being angry with," as Webster's cites. This is a conscious act.

It is interesting that the word *forgive* actually comes from the very ancient roots meaning "to give away." And that is actually what we do when we forgive. We give away our resentment, our anger. Think of it as leaning over a bridge railing above a fast-flowing stream and heaving your resentment and hatred over the edge to be carried away by the swirl of the waters.

3. *We become willing to bear the pain of another's sin against us.* The will is the part of the mind for which we bear responsibility. Like Kathy, we often bring it to reluctant obedience to Scripture. We cry, "I can't forgive, but I am willing to try." At this point we begin to understand and experience what it is like to be Christ, the One who gasped out, in the midst of his torture, "Father, forgive them, for they know not what they do" (Luke 23:34, RSV).

When the pain of our tormentor becomes real to us, and when we link it with our own willingness to take that pain and release the offender, we participate in a Godlike act and suddenly understand that forgiveness is costly. It was costly to Christ, who was willing to bear the pain, who willingly died, who willingly forgave, who instructed us to forgive seventy times seven.

Christ is willing—willing to bear the pain, the affront of every evil, hateful, disobedient, and selfish act you have committed. He asks that you be willing to do the same. At this point, forgiveness ceases to be simply doctrine and becomes a gripping experience.

4. *We wait for and expect God to work an act of release within.* Forgiveness is not complete until something supernatural occurs, until there is a work of release within us that could only be brought about by divine and holy action. Whenever

we are dealing with people struggling to forgive, we ask them to be willing to take the pain. Then we ask them to go to prayer and see the cross of Christ in their mind's eye. We ask them to carry their burden of pain to the foot of the cross and to leave it there. That is the reality of redemption.

Waiting bowed at the foot of this death-gibbet, our pain begins to ease, cleansing tears flow, and our constricted heart and soul loosen. A quiet inner peace grows, a gentle inner light warms us. We have understood Calvary; now we begin to experience Resurrection.

All normal psychological responses? Perhaps, but one day soon or down the road of years, we will begin to experience a surprising compassion for the crippled, hollow, half-people who did us such harm. Impossible? Humanly, yes. But not to God, not to God.

The watershed issue of Christianity that makes it distinctly different from all other world religions is this very issue. Can we love our enemies? Can we bless those who persecute us? Can we pray for those who despitefully use us? In our humanness we cannot. But God begins to fill us with his redemptive love. He frees us through forgiveness of the effect of evil practiced against us. He begins to fill us with something akin to compassion. And this we can only call a miracle.

I forgave my father and wrote him a note for the first time in years. Before receiving my letter, he called me to ask forgiveness. I could say I already had.

I forgave my mother and father yesterday. I still don't ever want to see them again; but at least I can live with the memory of what they did. And suddenly, I feel wonderful. What a relief!

I know now why my husband wept and wept before he died. My daughters told me he had sexually abused them. At first I cursed him in my heart, but then I repented. I

*think I have forgiven him. That man went to the grave
with these terrible acts on his soul.*

———————

*I forgave my abuser, and whereas before there was
scarcely a day I didn't remember, now there is scarcely
a day that I do.*

———————

*I forgave and felt such holy inner release. It was then I
understood that God was angry at them, too, but he still
loved them.*

Forgiveness is a choice. It can be dramatic; it can be slow
and barely recognizable. Either way, we notice that the pain
from the memory of the acts against us is diminishing. It is
often an ongoing process. There are many people we all have
had to forgive again and again. As one abuse survivor told
me, "I find I have to forgive each time I remember."

Often the subconscious mind stores the living realization
of past horrible acts so tightly that it needs to hear the words
of forgiveness spoken with authority in order to be convinced.
At this point, it may be extremely important that a trusted
person hear our words of repentance, our request for forgiveness. We humans often need to hear Christ's words of absolution, "Child, your sins are forgiven you," spoken by a loving
spiritual mentor. We often need a witness to hear our prayers
of forgiveness so that we can mark the time and the place and
say, "I know I have forgiven. I can remember the actual moment."

We may have to approach forgiveness feebly. Like Corrie
ten Boom, who met one of her cruel prison guards after World
War II, we may have to pray, "Jesus, I cannot forgive him.
Give me your forgiveness."[3] But the important thing is that
when we are faced with the need to forgive, we will learn to
forgive.

Lack of forgiveness is like a desk stacked with overdue,
unpaid bills. Through prayer therapy, we work our way down
through the stack. And with obedient practice, there comes a

time when we learn to pay the bill immediately when it comes due. We forgive as a spiritual discipline—when we are reminded of past pain, when the horrid words that wound are spoken, when someone tries to manipulate, to coerce, to use us. We forgive and are freed from the effect; and this freedom allows us to go about the process of rebuilding again the habitation of our interior, most sacred, human selves.

What Forgiveness Does for Us

Forgiveness is the only way in which we can simultaneously embrace and be free of our pasts. Until there is forgiveness, we are locked in a painful relationship with the person who has wronged us. Our living hatred and resentment of the person keeps him present even though it may be years since we have seen him. He may be completely removed from us and still continue to ruin our lives if we are bound to him by the cords of hatred. We are, after all, slaves to the persons we hate. When we forgive, we are released from this destructive bonding.

Forgiveness also opens us fully to the forgiveness God extends to us. "Forgive us our trespasses," we recite in the Lord's Prayer, *"as we forgive* those who trespass against us." Why this contingency?

If we think of the illustration of the household of the mind with rooms double-bolted and windows boarded, then we will have a good visual picture of the effect of sin on a human soul. Into those closed rooms we have shoved the guilt of our own sins, our bitterness, our hate, our vengeful spirits as well as the memory of the pain of grievous acts against us. Until we take the key of forgiveness and tentatively push it into one of those locks and (however reluctantly) open those doors, God's love is often unable to reach our most inward, wounded selves. God's light cannot shine through the dusty, shuttered windows with the shades pulled and the curtains drawn tight. All the Holy Spirit needs is one little crack, a closed thing pushed ever so slightly open, a faint cry—*I forgive.*

But God will not force the door. And for the abuse victim who has so often been encroached upon by force, that is an overwhelmingly precious reality. The Holy Spirit waits for an invitation to come into our most sacred inner selves. And at first, for many, "I forgive" is the closest thing to a welcome that can be given.

Look at all that forgiveness does:

1. When we "forgive those who trespass against us," we empty our hearts of hatred and make room for God's love and forgiveness.

2. When God forgives us, he is offering grace, not just as a gift for us to have and to hold, but in order that it may flow through us and onto others. By forgiving, we become channels of God's love in a love-starved world.

3. When we forgive, we act like Christ: We experience personal Gethsemanes and Golgothas. We walk the way of the Cross and share in fellowship with our Lord Jesus Christ. It is, for us, an act of obedience and of identification.

4. When we forgive, we open the festering wounds of our lives to the healing of God. As any medical person knows, only clean wounds can heal properly. That's why the first step in healing is cleansing—however painful that may be.

7
The Journey toward Healing

Kathy's Story

My initial sense of release lasted for several months. Then God began to work in my life to make me face things in greater detail. The overview had been taken care of, but now he and I had to take care of the details.

I began to be involved in intensive Bible study. Up until that point, I had been terribly addicted to the afternoon soaps on television. I would get all my work done so that by early afternoon I could be in the family room, maybe with mending or ironing to do, in front of the television. When I realized how unhelpful and unhealthy these shows were, and what a waste of time they were, I decided to give God the same amount of time that I had given to the soaps: three and a half hours every afternoon. I figured if I had been able to arrange my housework so I could watch the soaps, I could now arrange my housework to give me the same amount of time to learn the Scriptures.

At first, studying was very difficult for me. Although I had been a good student in the past, I did not find Bible study very easy nor, at first, particularly enjoyable. I was in such poor mental condition that concentration was hard, almost painful. I literally forced myself not to look ahead at the next question in the home-study course I was working on, lest it frighten me. I'd start in and I'd say, "Lord, just help me answer this one question." And then, when I'd get it done, I'd go on to the next one.

I literally prayed my way through each study, question by question. I started with an inductive study of Philippians, a short New Testament book. Later, as my knowledge and confidence and hunger for the Word grew, I went on to study some of the great biblical themes: God's nature, his covenants with us, and so on. Gradually, I was gaining a biblical and Christian mindset. My mind was being renewed.

There were, of course, practical implications of this new way of thinking. In my marriage. In my role as mother. In my poor self-image. For example, I was still overeating—probably a carryover from self-destructive urges. I did battle on that issue and lost about forty pounds. But it was—and still is—a battle to keep that in balance, using self-discipline but not becoming obsessed with the whole thing.

And meanwhile, I realized I had to go still deeper. A woman whom I met through the group Bible study pledged herself to me as a "prayer partner." We met regularly to pray together. The Scriptures teach, "Confess your sins to each other and pray for each other so that you may be healed" (James 5:16). I am learning that healing still comes that way.

Susan Forward says, "Revealing a major trauma . . . is just the beginning. . . . People sometimes find so much relief in the initial revelation that they leave treatment prematurely. . . . When the initial euphoria wears off, the patient is still struggling with unresolved conflicts. . . . Emotional purgings need to be experienced repeatedly."[1]

Psychologist and author M. Scott Peck notes that most abuse survivors "are simply seeking relief. When they realize they are going to be challenged as well as supported, many flee and others are tempted to flee."[2]

Like many child sexual abuse survivors, Kathy is still experiencing an ongoing healing—an initial dramatic release followed by a sense of still needing deeper freedom from the bondage of the past. We often tell those who have had initial spiritual encounters that these incredible moments are God's promises of what the future can be. It is not for us to look back when life becomes difficult again and whine, "But God, why? You were so close and I was so free—what happened?" Rather we have a gift to hold to our hearts, a memory of beauty to make bearable the plunge into a past that continues to strangle our present.

Kathy's determination, her psychological understanding, and the faithfulness of a friend who listened to moments dark with pain and grief are remarkable. Her intense interaction with Scripture and determined prayer are tools that can be used by other abuse survivors. It is possible that one day Kathy may even discover a desire for a sustained exchange in a professional therapeutic environment—or she may not. But her determined commitment to growth assures steady, healthy results.

Other voices recognize that maturity can be achieved only through sometimes arduous progress. And very realistically, many women recognize that while they have had and are experiencing healing, there are still scars.

I am healing, a baby-step at a time.

After three years of serious marriage problems, we went to a Marriage Encounter weekend. My husband accepted Christ, and I am on the road to slow healing.

I was an abused child, and although the Lord has given me great healing and an understanding marriage partner, I know the scars of my early experience are still with me.

I was abused as a child for about fifteen years by my father and brother. The scars will be with me until I see Christ.

The lack of understanding on the part of fellow Christians with regard to the length and depth of this healing process is often a frustration to the survivor determined to discover permanent wholeness. But the voices also tell of discovering in Christ a rare intimacy (perhaps they have come to experience him as one of the few males who can be totally trusted) and an understanding that others are unable to give.

> *I find only too often people think you are living in the past when you speak of it. . . . People say, "You should be over that by now."*

> *The sexual abuse in my childhood was severe, and often my world shifted into cycles of unreality. Strangely enough, the one reality I can remember that always held (even when I was a little child) was Christ. I don't know how this happened or why especially to me—all I know is that when things were most confusing, he was there. He is still the Center.*

A Time for Healing

Healing can be instantaneous for some; many testify to spiritually cathartic moments that hastened them toward health, allowing them to bypass certain developmental steps. But most of the time, healing is deliberate and orderly. It helps to keep in mind the analogy of physical healing. While a scratch or a sprained ankle heals relatively quickly, the multiple injuries caused by a terrible accident can take months, if not years, to mend. The impact may have shattered bones, torn internal organs. First come sessions of delicate surgery. The patient is not whole when wheeled out of the operating room. Then comes a long period of recovery: the slow knitting together of flesh, muscle, ligament; the multiplication of new cells; the removing of the old, traumatized ones. Both the wounds inflicted by the accident and the incisions made by invasive surgery must heal.

Healing takes time. Often the expectation for quick healing from the effects of early child sexual trauma is unrealistic. It is just as simplistic as thinking: Why do I have to have this tumor removed? Why won't it just go away? Why do I have to take penicillin for double pneumonia? I hate medicine. Won't I get better if I just get plenty of rest?

Some survivors want to get well without cooperating with the natural healing processes that the Divine Healer has built into the human psyche. Damage from early child sexual abuse, from incest, is often enormous. It is also reparable. Perhaps that truth needs to be repeated. *It is also reparable.* But there must be an attitude of help-seeking on the part of the wounded one. Jesus still asks us, as he asked the paralyzed man beside the pool of Bethesda, "Do you want to get well?" (John 5:6). In a very real sense, it is up to us.

When asked how we could motivate a woman to come for help, a sexual assault counselor observed, "Women like this have had so little control of their lives that it is important that they act autonomously in seeking help. All you can do is tell them of the help available and offer your support in getting to it. Then they must act on their own behalf. If they don't we can't help them anyhow."

God usually does not help us toward health until we take one step, one action that indicates serious decision, serious desire to be well, on our part. We must seek healing at whatever level we are at—even if we can offer no more than a faint, desperate gasp, "Oh, God, help!"

We begin to walk—crawl, creep, strain—toward the light, like Kathy going past a Christian friend's house, going to a Bible study, seeking out a pastor, attending a women's conference.

At some point, the individual must commit herself to the rehabilitation process. The lack of this commitment is like the child shaking his head at the teaspoon of medicine, clamping his mouth shut, spitting out the tablet, or purposefully gagging while swallowing the capsule. Without a cooperative leaning toward health, we are like little children still waiting for someone to do it for us, to take care of us, to make it all better. God does it with us and works through others on our behalf, but we must take some initiative toward health on our own. Deciding to seek counseling or psychotherapy is one of the hardest yet most courageous and significant decisions an individual can make.

The Determination Factor

After physical injury, atrophied muscles must be exercised, rebuilt limbs must be painfully stretched and flexed, sometimes nervous signal systems must be repatterned in order for the body and brain to coordinate. Whenever world-class sports events are shown on television, there is the inevitable story about the championship athlete who last year suffered a terrible injury or broke a leg in a skiing accident. "We thought he would be scratched from this season's competition," some newscaster invariably comments. The cameras then focus on scenes in physical therapy rooms showing the determined skier working out for hours on weight machines under the hovering attention of a medical sports therapist, building again the traumatized bones and muscles. To the whole world's surprise (the part of the world that is interested at any rate), the athlete appears in this year's skiing circuit, better than ever.

This determined action is what we must bring to the search for emotional wholeness; we must learn to grit our teeth and say, "I will be well." We must expect that God will become the surgeon who excises the malignancy of the past that threatens to spread in our souls. He will use many means in this operation—Scripture, the inner light of the Holy Spirit, loving Christians, skilled non-Christians, groups of incest survivors, the offices of the church. Healing, no matter in what form it comes, is always a part of God's plan for us.

And after this holding of hands, this task that requires the rich interplay between human love and divine intervention and help, we grit our teeth and say, "I will be well, so help me God."

Divine Therapy

God is also the Divine Therapist who oversees our rehabilitation, whose hand is available for us to squeeze when the pain becomes unbearable, who makes sure if we trust ourselves to him that we won't be plunged into therapy more demanding than we can possibly sustain. But God also insists that if we are going to compete in the circuit of life's championship experiences, we must sweat, strain, and work out under his rehabilitation program.

The apostle Paul wrote the following to the Christians in the ancient city of Corinth:

> Do you not know that the unrighteous will not inherit the kingdom of God? Do not be deceived; neither the immoral, nor idolators, nor adulterers, nor [homosexuals], nor thieves, nor the greedy, nor drunkards, nor revilers, nor robbers will inherit the kingdom of God. *And such were some of you.* But you were washed, you were sanctified, you were justified in the name of the Lord Jesus Christ and in the Spirit of our God. (1 Corinthians 6:9-11, RSV, italics added)

At first glance, these verses may seem discouraging to the survivors of early child sexual abuse, who are hounded by self-blame and self-hate. Many survivors will immediately fixate on the negative phrases—"the unrighteous will not inherit"—and actually miss this Scripture's tremendous positive implications for them.

In the moral confusion of a sexually perverted Corinthian society, Paul gives powerful hope: "And such were some of you. *But you were washed* (made clean), *you were sanctified* (set apart as holy for God's special use), *you were justified* (made as though you had never sinned)." No one who wants to be whole, to be restored, to remember innocence again is beyond the circle of God's healing power. *"And such were some of you."*

> *I was molested and raped as a child. I've been into drugs and drinking. All my life I have felt dirty and worthless and no good, and was told that all my life. I'm middle-aged and I'm still feeling this. I'm going to group counseling and that has helped, but I need to know how God sees me. I'm crying out to God for help.*

Help comes when the abuse survivor learns how to put herself in the way of God's healing grace.

The Mind Renewed

To the Christians in Rome, people living out their faith in another morally depraved city, Paul writes, "Do not conform any longer to the pattern of this world, but be transformed by the renewing of your mind. Then you will be able to test and approve what God's will is—his good, pleasing and perfect will" (Romans 12:2).

How can our minds be renewed?

1. *Scripture*. Modern social scientists have written extensively about positive behavior modification, but the Scripture has been teaching spiritual principles of attitude and behavior modification for centuries. One step toward health that abuse survivors need to take is a renewal of their minds. God's desire for them is that they will be able to focus on what is good (not what is ugly) and acceptable (not what is socially and morally degrading) and perfect (what is whole).

Kathy has given us an excellent model for beginning this process—a saturation of her mind with Scripture and a participation in intensive prayer therapy. For many, however, emulating Kathy's hours and dedication will seem a mountain too rugged to climb; some women and men are overwhelmed just with the effort of living out one more day.

Be still and know that I am God. Although unaware that these words were from Scripture, Kathy clung to them like a lifeline tossed to save her from drowning.

Often mind renewal begins with bite-sized portions, a Scripture phrase repeated over and over, a verse memorized to hold off the threatening darkness. Footholds are chiseled into the mountain; handholds are discovered; we slip and grab at a strongly rooted sapling: "The law of the Lord is perfect, reviving the soul." We rest on a sheltering ledge: "The statutes of the Lord are trustworthy, making wise the simple." We pant, we stave off the anxiety attack from the fear of falling: "The precepts of the Lord are right, giving joy to the heart." We sleep awhile. We wake. We start the difficult ascent again: "The commands of the Lord are radiant, giving light to the eyes" (Psalm 19:7-8).

I now read the Bible every morning and every night and

> *try to learn one verse a day out of my reading, for one's*
> *thoughts can go back to the ruts very easily if one doesn't*
> *have a full armor of strength to keep them out.*

For many, it is only after this gentle, beginning rehabilitation with the Word of God in the survivor's battered and exhausted mind that she develops the capacity to do more. She joins a Bible study. She turns off the afternoon soaps and works through a Bible studyguide. She writes out verses on three-by-five cards and tapes them to the bathroom mirror, the refrigerator, the dashboard of the car. She begins to discover that Scripture is the ointment that anesthetizes the sting of wounds. It is the balm, the oil that eases pain, the antibiotic that fights raging inner soul disease. One simple phrase can ease the mind's torment. One memorized passage can obliterate the on-again, off-again fixation with suicide. "He sent his word to heal them and bring them alive out of the pit of death" (Psalm 107:20, NEB).

Renewing the mind has its full effect when, like Kathy, we can give ourselves to intensive study. In fact, there is a direct relationship between the effectiveness of the rehabilitation process and the amount of time we can give to Scripture. John White writes in *Masks of Melancholy:*

> An area where the pastoral counselor can offer help . . .
> is to teach and to encourage the sufferers in solid, in-
> ductive Bible study. . . . Years ago, when I was seriously
> depressed, the thing that saved my own sanity was a
> dry-as-dust grappling with Hosea's prophecy. I spent
> weeks, morning by morning, making meticulous notes,
> checking historical allusions in the text. Slowly I began
> to sense the ground under my feet growing steadily
> firmer. I knew without any doubt that healing was con-
> stantly springing from my struggle to grasp the meaning
> of the prophecy.[3]

2. *Prayer.* Kathy worked through each agonizing memory of her past in the presence of a prayer partner. This kind of prayer work has enormous efficacy. Very often psychological

healings that we have seen have come more quickly when the abuse survivor found a good psychological counselor who believed in and used prayer in the therapeutic process. But again, this plunge into the pain may be overwhelming to many who have spent their entire lives avoiding the memory of their sexually abused past.

> *The Lord Jesus Christ and I work on these things from the past as I can handle the knowledge. From the very beginning I showed myself and the Lord my expanse for rage—but my true desire is to love people, the Lord's creations, to love truth and knowledge. I hate this dark, covered-up side of myself, but the Lord knows how to reveal the darkness to me.*

Like Bible study, prayer may be exercised in extended periods of time or in tiny life-spaces. Those who are coping with looming emotional instability may only be able to take prayer in small doses. Perhaps the following ways of praying may prove helpful.

a. Feeling prayer. A simple form (daily, if possible) might begin with how you feel: "God, today I feel so lonely. Does anyone understand my pain?" Then start listing hoped-for minimal achievements for the day—"I would like to get a decent meal on the table. I would like to spend fifteen minutes reading Scripture. I would like to go to the store without having a panic attack. I would like to go through the day without screaming at the children."

At the end of each day, look back on it. Now is the time for *reviewing prayer.* Thank God for his help. Write down the small victories. "Today was better. I woke this morning and felt hope. I now finally know that you love me. I want someday soon to feel your love."

b. Listening prayer. The second type of prayer we recommend for abuse victims is the prayer of listening. In a later chapter we will describe this more fully. In its essence, listening prayer is so simple there is no excuse not to practice it. It is nothing more, really, than sitting before the Lord, becoming aware of his existence through a Bible passage, or going to a place filled with quietude, and then hushing one's noisy heart and saying, "Lord, what is it you have to say to me today? Here I am."

Most people can't hear God's subtle, inward voice because they are so busy crying out, so noisily demanding things from God that they never take time to hear him speak softly to them. They are like the child downstairs who comes home from school screaming, "Mom! Mom! Hey, Mom!" And each time he calls, the mother, who is upstairs answers, "I'm up here! Here I am! Up here!" But the child can't hear his mother's answer above his own shouts.

Sometimes we hear nothing after we have quieted our noisy child-cries. But the silence begins to seep into our souls. Sometimes the quiet is interrupted by brain chatter—*You forgot to take out the meat to defrost; You forgot to call so-and-so*. Write these notes down to free your mind from worry and quiet yourself again. Sometimes then you'll hear God's quiet word, "My Beloved." That is well worth waiting for.

Answers to the questions "What shall I do? To whom shall I turn? Where can I find help?" are often found in silence. Our problem as people is not that we don't ask the questions, not that we don't cry out; but most often it is that we don't listen enough for a reply.

c. A prayer journal. Writing out prayers makes the spiritual journey concrete. It records the mind's sometimes small but nevertheless significant renewal. In fact, one counselor we know never agrees to counsel with an abuse victim unless she will agree to journal. Journaling is one of the methods by which we begin to achieve self-directed spiritual and emotional growth. Recording your prayers can be an extension of the journaling process we have already encouraged you to begin.

Prayer—how often the voices of survivors link it to healing. An elderly man, abused as a child, spent a lifetime struggling with guilt.

> *I was led to John 14:27—"Peace I leave with you; my peace I give you. I do not give as the world gives. Do not let your hearts be troubled and do not be afraid."*

After a long prayer upon my knees unto God I felt his peace from the top of my head to my toes, and my life has never been the same since. My guilt was removed then.

A Christian couple lifted me in prayer for many months. Then through a Christian outreach ministry, I was led to a seminar on depression. Through many prayers I was delivered from the bondage of abuse.

Two years ago the Lord brought a dear friend into my life as a daily telephone prayer partner, spending ten to fifteen minutes most weekday mornings in prayer over the phone. Finally, I was able to confide in her about my dad, after I found out she had been raped in her childhood. A true healing process had begun as we prayed and cried together.

What an incredible network of love the prayer net is. Do any of us really utilize its healing potential?

Perhaps you might begin in prayer by praying daily, "All I know of myself I offer to all that I know of you." Write it down. Make it concrete.

Something You Can Do Right Now

Choose a Bible verse or passage that gives you the reassurance you most need. Write the Scripture out on a card that you can tape to a place where you will see it often. Here are some Scriptures for you to meditate on:

1. To help you deal with anxiety: Philippians 4:6; Matthew 6:25-32
2. To help you deal with guilt: 1 John 1:9-10; 1 John 2:1-2; Isaiah 43:25
3. To help you know God's love: Romans 5:4-5; 1 John 1–5; John 15:1-17
4. To help you gain assurance of salvation: Romans 10:9-11; John 3:16
5. To help you sense your worth as a person: Psalm 139

You have listened as God speaks to you in his Word. Now answer the Lord. Express you heart's response in words, in a notebook or in the space below.

Mother Teresa describes prayer this way:

> The beginning of prayer is silence, . . . God speaking in the silence of the heart. And then we start talking to God from the fullness of our hearts. And he listens. The beginning of prayer is Scripture, . . . we listen to God speaking. And then we begin to speak to him again from the fullness of our hearts. And he listens. That is really prayer. Both sides listening and both sides speaking.[4]

And for the abuse survivor, prayer—both sides listening and both sides speaking—and Scripture, sent to heal and deliver from the pit of death, are the beginning of the renewing of the mind.

8
Thinking Straight about God

Kathy's Story

I had to come to a new understanding of God. My initial search was really to find out what I could about the character of God. I remember studying the attributes of God—justice, holiness, righteousness, omnipresence, omniscience. I studied what each of these words means and began to see what a great God he is.

I studied the sovereignty of God. I came to believe that God's perfect sovereignty could have prevented what happened to me when I was five years old. That God chose not to intervene has to be because he ultimately purposed that good should come about despite the evil that was done to me.

To be very honest, from where I am right now in the healing process, I can say I'm not even sorry that it happened because I have seen the grace of God in a marvelous way. And God has taught me so much. I no longer have the self-pitying, "Why me? Why did I have to have my life messed up by someone else?" attitude. I have learned that God's grace is greater than what happened to me, and that makes the big difference.

In my teenage years and early twenties I used to think, *No male is ever going to dominate me.* I was not in any feminist groups, but my attitudes were certainly consonant with theirs.

So coming to terms with a masculine God was very important for me.

When you have been through child sexual abuse, you have no respect for males. You don't trust them. So it's important to your healing to come to trust this masculine God; to honor him, to submit to him. The last thing a woman who's been defiled by a man wants is to be submissive to a man. Everything in you wants to fight men. To stand up against them. All of them.

But when you come to the Word of God, you have to come as an individual before God and submit. You have to honor him and respect him. And in the process, your perception of males is corrected. "They" are no longer the enemy. Evil is the real enemy.

It's all quite circular and very important for redeveloping relationships. As you learn to love and trust God, you are healed in your ability to love and trust your own husband. You stop being hostile to men in their maleness.

Beyond Gender

Kathy resolved her conflict with males and maleness by coming to embrace the God of the Bible, overwhelmingly depicted in masculine terminology and addressed by the name of "Father." Other abuse survivors have found comfort in discovering that the God of the Bible, who transcends human gender, also demonstrates the tender, nurturant qualities that are often thought of as feminine. Consider this:

> In homemaking I share in the very nature of God in many ways. I think of the Lord Jesus saying tenderly, "I go to prepare a place for you" (John 14:2). Jesus is homemaking for us—preparing an atmosphere where love can flourish eternally. Washing and cleaning are godlike functions. It is God the Holy Spirit who undertakes "the washing of regeneration" (Titus 3:5). . . . I think of the Lord Jesus Christ preparing a bride for himself, "not having spot, or wrinkle, or any such thing" (Ephesians 5:27).

> As I make the decisions regarding clothing for my
> family, . . . I am reminded of the One who robes us in
> his own righteousness, and someday will clothe us in
> "fine linen, clean and white" (Revelation 19:8). Meal-
> making, too, is something which is done by the Good
> Shepherd, who "prepares a table before me in the pres-
> ence of my enemies" (Psalm 23:5). And as I tidy and
> straighten the house, I recall that "God is not the author
> of confusion, but of peace" (1 Corinthians 14:33).[1]

Not only does the Bible picture God performing roles frequently assigned by society to women, but God is also spoken
of in feminine metaphors: as the mother eagle who comes
under her fledglings and carries them on her strong wings
(Deuteronomy 32:11); as the desert woman spreading her sheltering tent (Psalm 61:4); as the lap and breasts where we
quieten ourselves like little children (Psalm 131). For the
abuse survivor, some of these pictures may create access to
love and trust that are not available to them through masculine
language or imagery.

Rightly understood, God's selfhood transcends human categories of sexuality or gender. Language reflects masculine and
feminine traits and pronouns not because God is sexual—
either masculine or feminine—but because we cannot imagine
personhood in other than gendered terms. A full vision of God
as revealed in the Bible includes both fatherly strength and
motherly nurturance. Abuse survivors find healing for their
own broken self-image and their fractured image of masculine
and feminine humanity in a contemplation of the steadfast love
of a God who, unlike all the gods of the pagan panoplies, is
beyond genital activity and sexual identification.

Rebuilding Worldviews Shattered by Abuse

> *I'm a Christian, but I feel that God hates me, and without
> him there's no meaning to life. Maybe I'm not even a
> Christian.*

I'm saved, but it took me twelve years to realize that God could really love me, and many times I still struggle with that.

I was the victim of abuse in my "Christian" family. Although I have worked through much of my past, the issue of Christianity and what it really means has continued to be a major problem for me.

I (Maxine) was talking with Edie, a young mother whose childhood had been full of the fear of displeasing her abusive, perfectionist father. "God's intentions toward you are loving," I reassured her. "He has good plans for you."

"Oh, I know," she answered quickly. "Just as long as I don't botch them up."

In that momentary exchange, I glimpsed how difficult the matter of trust, of God's unconditional love, was for her. She had transferred her father's negative perfectionism to God. God would do good things for her, all right, but only contingent on her own efforts. In this bondage, she was trying to work out both the painful past and the stress-laden present.

Throughout childhood, we build our worldview by assimilating thousands of bits of information and building them into the framework by which we understand and adapt to the world around us. Theologians are paying increasing attention to the family unit as "the cradle of theology."[2]

And small wonder that Jesus told us to become as little children in order to enter the kingdom. Childlike trust is an essential ingredient in spiritual faith. Survivors of child sexual abuse need to completely rebuild their worldviews. They need to construct a mental model in which the father figure, or often any authority figure, is trustworthy. In doing this they create a framework for real faith in God as he really is.

Child sexual abuse within the family is a form of blasphemy. It breaks the image of God in the child. "So God created man in his own image, in the image of God he created him; male and female he created them" (Genesis 1:27). Sexual abuse within the family shatters the understanding that God is like my loving father who protects me, wants the best for me, disciplines me wisely when I am wrong, loves me utterly and always in what I am and in what I am becoming. The incestuous sex act interrupts and wretchedly confuses the progression from accepting healthy human love to knowing the divine love of God. As one victim said, "What's a father? A father's just a name, no more than a name."

What Is God Like?

The nature and characteristics of God are the main theme of Scripture from Genesis to Revelation. The God who very specifically warned the Hebrew people not to make any engraved or pictured image of God, chose to reveal himself in words—words that would be translated and passed through the centuries so that each generation can build, from the words of Scripture, a picture of God which is true to his self-revelation. How can we relate to a God we do not know? Immersing ourselves in Scripture to acquaint ourselves with it is immensely helpful to personal renewal.

Kathy speaks of coming to terms with the sovereignty of God, and the theological concept that God rules as a divine and absolute authority, overseeing the entire cosmos. Every Christian must grapple with the reality of this theology. A. W. Tozer says, "God's sovereignty is the attribute by which he rules his entire creation, and to be sovereign God must be all-knowing, all-powerful, and absolutely free. . . . The sovereignty of God is a fact well established in the Scriptures and declared aloud by the logic of truth."[3]

We must understand that God has decreed humanity free to choose and has given us a moral responsibility for that choice. God's sovereignty also ordained that humanity's choice for evil will not derail God's plan for good for his creation.

Christ came into our wounded world to partake of our brokenness. As we press into his pierced hands the pain we have experienced because of the evil choices of others, we undergo an amazing, divine alchemy in which the evil that has happened to us is able to have ultimately good results for us.

It was that way for Joseph, betrayed and sold by his own brothers. Years later, after rejection and temptation and imprisonment and abandonment, after refusing to succomb to the seductions of money, sex, and power, he became the chief advisor to Pharaoh, the second in command of the land of Egypt. Facing his own brothers, who had come to beg for food to sustain their families during a desperate famine, he was finally able to say, "It was not you who sent me here, but God. . . . You intended to harm me, but God intended it for good" (Genesis 45:8, 50:20).

These words are like Kathy's amazing comments, "I'm not even sorry that it happened because I have seen the grace of God in a marvelous way. . . . I don't know if I would undo the past if I could." In both Joseph's and Kathy's lives something miraculous happened. When God redeems pain and uses healed scars, he shows himself as he really is. Even the memory of past abuse can be used by God as a tool for the healing of others. History is full of the testimonies of people who, like Joseph and Kathy, have discovered the real God.

Without going into complex theological explanations, let us suggest a beginning place in this journey to discover the true nature of a real God.

Learning about God through Christ

God has revealed himself in words; he has also revealed himself in the New Testament in a person, Jesus of Nazareth, who lived out his Father's original plan for what the human was designed to be. Jesus showed us in flesh the divine image. "No one has ever seen God, but God the One and Only [the only begotten Son], who is at the Father's side, has made him known" (John 1:18). Christ is the ultimate man.

We can understand why women who have been hurt by men want to relate to a feminized God; but it is this man—man as God intended man to be—who can bring healing to the woman who learns to relate to him. Jesus teaches us to call God our "Father," and he demonstrates and teaches that God is a holy and trustworthy heavenly Father (one who does not creep into the room at night, who does not coerce perverted activity, whose footsteps don't sound in the hallway), a Father who encourages our growth at every point—physical, spiritual, mental, and social.

Certainly God transcends the human categories of "male" and "female"; yet when we remove the masculine names for God from Scripture and liturgy, we depersonalize him. As the attempt is made to create an androgynous model, contact with God's intimate personality is lost.

God has revealed himself to us as a Person. Although sometimes using feminine descriptions of himself (Christ said he was like a mother hen who would gather her chicks under her wings), he has declared his personhood in terms that are overwhelmingly masculine. We are most often invited to relate to him as Father, as Lover, as Husband. Rather than changing the vocabulary of the Bible, we need to rethink our views of what maleness is all about so that we will be able to relate to God through the powerful verbal metaphors by which he has pictured himself for us.

The place to begin this journey is with the male Christ, who is a man unlike any other.

A woman described a journey to the Far East:

> The Buddhist monks surprised me. They grabbed their robes away from women in public places lest they be defiled. We couldn't hand them anything directly but had to pass it first to a mediary or place an object on the ground. Our training manual insisted: Don't sit on the same seat of a bus where the monks sit. A monk cannot sit next to you. In sharing a taxi upcountry, there must be a male sitting between you and a monk. Make it easy for monks to pass you in crowded areas, holding your skirt close to your body if necessary. It made me feel positively unclean.

When we encounter the misogyny (hatred of women) of certain vengeful mullahs and males with similar attitudes in our Western religious holy orders, our hearts are filled with fear. We think of Christ, another holy man, and of how he came into just such a male-dominated society and began to relate to women in ways unlike any other man had related to them.

Christ had created woman, he understood her, he had compassion on her, and he invited her to partake of his life and work.

The Gospel of Womanhood

The book of Luke has been called "The Gospel of Womanhood." His Gospel opens with accounts of three remarkable women of faith: Elizabeth, who bears a child in her old age and raises him with such diligent care that Christ himself says, "among those born of women there is no one greater than John"; Mary, who submits to the overwhelming task of becoming mother to the promised Messiah, "Behold, I am the handmaid of the Lord; let it be to me according to your word"; and Anna, the eighty-four-year-old mystic who never left the temple, worshiping, fasting, and praying there night and day.

Having set the stage with these three remarkable women, Luke continues to weave together the amazing variety and peculiarities of the people who populated the life of Christ. Women are not dominant in this book but they are prominent. Christ's attitude toward them was chaste and tender and filled with consideration, a radical approach considering the culture of his time, which decreed that women were unworthy to receive education, unable to function as legal witnesses, and worthless in contrast with their male peers. Actually, Jesus' open, brotherly attitude is still radical. There are few churchmen who can emulate Christ's purity toward women or his regard for them. Certainly, none can match his sacrifice. Listen to Luke. Learn more about Christ and his women friends through this historical writer.

Here comes a widow. Her son is dead and she weeps, all alone in the world, with no one to support her; even her husband's family name is dead. Christ has compassion on her and raises her son to life. Is there any group more overlooked in our society than the older widow?

Here comes the town whore, a common woman of the streets. Weeping, she dares to embrace his feet. She washes them with her tears and wipes them dry with her hair. The company of self-righteous, indignant dignitaries look on askance. What does Christ do with this prostitute? He accepts her weeping adoration. Her tears do not embarrass him. He refuses to humiliate her before the shocked onlookers. He forgives her sins. One of the highest suicide rates in our society is among prostitutes. Christ does not repudiate these women but turns toward them in compassion.

Christ lovingly heals Peter's mother-in-law. Can you imagine Jesus cracking a mother-in-law joke? We can't.

Who are these who travel with him from town to town and bake his bread? Who are these who through their husbands' business contacts or wealth advance his public ministry? Aren't these the neurotic middle-aged women, with their emotional and psychological disorders—Joanna, Susanna, Magdalene, and many other nameless women whom Luke describes?

Here comes a woman with a "female disease." She says she has had a flow of blood for twelve years and her condition has made her a temple pariah, levitically unclean. Some doctors speculated that her problem was psychological. Some treated her condition symptomatically. All gladly accepted her payment of their fees. Now she touches the hem of Jesus' robe. She feels too unclean to dare to ask for or deserve his public attention. She is ashamed of her humiliating, malfunctioning woman's body. What if he turns on her as the other holy men have?

But Christ feels her tentative tug in the jostling crowd; he knows a seeker's touch. He makes her declare before all the people that she has been healed. No more rumor or innuendo

---

Something You Can Do Right Now

Turn to the Gospel of Luke in the New Testament. There is an old meditative form called "Christic meditation" that is practiced by looking deeply into a scriptural passage and interacting with the Christ revealed in that passage.

Walk into the events as you read, as though you were actually present. See the setting, the sea, the people, the little towns, the temple pavement. Now move yourself into the historical scriptural setting, taking all your needs into that event involving the Lord.

For instance, turn to Luke 8:40 where the account of the healing of the woman with an issue of blood is recorded. Can you understand her fearful hesitancy? Her desperation? Do you know what it is like to be unclean? In

here—she has been healed! In front of the townsfolk who have unsympathetically misunderstood her condition, he calls her "daughter" and publicly commends her faith and sends her away with his blessing of peace.

What a man this is!

Christ alludes to women in his teaching. His parables and real-life encounters are full of female prototypes—the importunate widow, the housewife who has lost one of her ten coins, the widow who places everything she has in the treasury—an example to stingy, wealthy givers. He refers to historical women as sermon illustrations—Lot's wife, a negative illustration, and the Queen of the South, a positive example of faith. He becomes women's advocate by insisting that a man is not to divorce his wife and take another; he is angry at men's capricious power and their degradation of women. He is the champion of women who suffer from such abandonment and rejection.

Even on the *via dolorosa* to his own crucifixion, bleeding and wounded, he stops to sympathize with the women who are weeping for him: "Daughters of Jerusalem, do not weep for me; weep for yourselves and for your children." He knows the terrible future of loss and destruction, rape and pillage which are in store for them all.

Luke records the women who watch at the crucifixion. He tells us that it was to these faithful ones, still attempting to minister to Jesus' mauled body with burial spices, that the glorious first message of resurrection was delivered.

---

your mind, do what she did. Slip painfully into the crowd, touch the fringe of his garment. See Christ in that event, a young man, mobbed by needy people, already on his way to heal a dying child, led on by a distraught father—but he takes time to search for you. What does he ask of you and what do you answer?

Work your way unhurriedly through the whole gospel of Luke. The Holy Spirit will use these Scriptures to surprise you with the living reality of a Christ who understands what it means to be a woman, a damaged woman, and who reaches out in love from almost every page. He will not neglect you; he will not abandon you; he will never abuse you or humiliate you.

You must meet this Man Christ!

One of our favorite passages about Christ is Mark 3:31-35. This again deals with Christ's relationship with women. "And his mother and his brothers came; and standing outside they sent to him and called him. . . . 'Your mother and brothers are outside, asking for you.' And he replied, 'Who are my mother and brothers?' And looking around on those who sat about him, he said, 'Here are my mother and my brothers! Whoever does the will of God is my brother, and sister, and mother' " (RSV).

There are many times when we've thought of Christ as our trustworthy older Brother who regards us with respect; one to whom we can turn when some of our human brothers in the church batter us with misguided theology. We have heard him speak from the pages of Scripture, "My little sister . . ." Renewing your mind with a knowledge of the true God, *as he really is,* may be the most exciting journey into wholeness you will ever take. Again, write down the things you learn, the inner thoughts guided by the Holy Spirit, the changes that occur. Miraculously, one day you too may be able to say, "You intended it to harm me, but God intended it for good, to accomplish what is now being done, the saving of many lives."

9
Self-Forgiveness, Self-Acceptance

Kathy's Story

With my ongoing quest for knowledge of God and the extensive healing I had received through forgiving and being forgiven, I experienced a period of euphoria that I thought would be mine forever. But then I again began to experience accusation and self-doubt. My past life made me very vulnerable to Satan. Even when you have settled it with God, the "accuser of the brethren" comes along and whispers doubts. How could God have forgiven you for all that?

I kept fighting back with teachings from the Word of God, but I finally realized that some things had been dealt with only on a surface level, and I was in need of a deeper healing than I had yet known.

I had forgiven my abuser. I knew God had forgiven me. But there was one important aspect that I had overlooked. *I had not genuinely forgiven myself.* You hear so much about accepting God's forgiveness and letting God help you forgive the other individual—but not too much is said about forgiving yourself.

What I decided to do was this: I asked my prayer partner if she would work with me on this new, deeper level of healing I needed. We decided to go back through each circumstance of my life and work through childhood memories that were still painful.

Prior to five years ago, there was little I could even recall. But beginning with my molestation, we went prayerfully to the very first circumstance involving my uncle and myself. Just to get to where I could face that event, we had to spend five or six afternoons in prayer together. With each incident I remembered, I reentered the situation and told the Lord what I was feeling. Then I asked him to forgive me for any feelings in me that were wrong. I also asked God to forgive the other person involved with me. And then, before God, I announced, as we completed praying through each scene, "And I forgive myself."

I asked the Lord by his Holy Spirit to reveal memories that needed healing. Many times I actually felt within my body the physical reactions of that long-ago moment. It was a painful process, but very worthwhile. And even though I had already forgiven in the broad sense, I felt the need to give and receive forgiveness with a witness for each remembered incident.

After each scene had been revisited and I had said, "God forgive him. God forgive me. I forgive myself. On the basis of your Word (1 John 1:9), I claim that you have faithfully and justly forgiven and cleansed me," I would then go on to the next circumstance and do exactly the same thing. With every young man that I could remember being with, I confessed my sin and again claimed 1 John 1:9. My prayer partner and I worked through my life right up to that very day.

Now, with a witness to my confession, I laid claim to God's promise of complete pardon and cleansing. I suddenly found I had strengthened my defense against the accuser. Now, when I sensed accusation, I could say, "I have dealt with that before God. I have dealt with that before my sister in Christ. She is my witness. And God is my witness. You have no basis on which to bring me into judgment."

With this prayer work done, I could continue with what has been a long and slow process for me: learning to accept myself; learning, even, to *like* myself.

The abuse survivor moves into life with her self-worth really destroyed. That is something I still have to work on. Because I'd been violated as a person, I questioned everything about myself. When you've been used and abused, you feel you are of no worth to anybody—other than to be used. So self-acceptance has got to be one of the hardest struggles. Forgiving the abuser, learning to think straight about God—those things seem to come easier. But I have to continuously work on self-acceptance, reaffirming that I am a person of value and accepted before God.

You have to learn to see yourself as an individual created in the image of God, marred most certainly by sin, but still an individual created uniquely for God's special purposes. It's a strange thing. Your husband can say, "I love you, I love you, I love you," and all you think is, *How could he love me?* It's not enough to live on another person's estimate of your worth— although I'm sure it helps. You've got to come to accept yourself.

Forgiving Ourselves

Perhaps the most difficult act of forgiving and the most critical one for the abuse survivor is learning to forgive herself. She must forgive herself with the same determination with which she forgives those who have brought her pain. A whole jury of self-accusations cries out against her: Why didn't I get help? Why didn't I say "No!"? Why did I compound my plight with acts of emotional self-mutilation? Why didn't I accept the truth sooner?—perhaps I could have salvaged my marriage, raised my children better. What is wrong with me? How can anyone stand me? How can I stand myself?

When we talk with victims of child abuse who now carry not only the displaced guilt of the truly guilty perpetrator but also struggle with the weighty baggage of self-hate, we remind them that they are a lot like a little child who was introduced to a dope habit early in life. Some adult injected a small dose of heroin into the child's vein, continually increasing the dosage until a dependency had been created. Of course the child enjoyed the drug-induced high, loved the effusive moments, craved other injections. Of course, the child now has to deal with the effects of that addiction, the insatiable need for more, the days lost to stupor, the cycle of physical and emotional highs and lows, the humiliating ugliness of withdrawal.

But the culpability, the true guilt, the error, was on the part of that adult who stabbed the needle into the child's skin and injected the first dose, then the next, then the next. The child is not responsible for that adult's action.

Child sexual abuse is the same. You are struggling against the symptoms of withdrawal from an act (or acts) perpetrated against you of which you were innocent. There is a confusing welter of causes and consequences, *but you were not guilty in that first act.* This realization can become a foundation on which you can lay the other bricks of self-forgiveness.

Begin by saying aloud the words, "I forgive myself." Forgive yourself for the moments that were *not* your responsibility but for which you have held yourself in judgment. Deal in confession with those actions that *are* your responsibility: your hatred, resentment, and bitterness; your sinful lifestyle; your vindictive "taking it out" on the people around you.

Take some quiet time and write out the specifics:

- "I confess and forgive myself for searching for love in promiscuity."
- "I forgive myself for trying to punish my parents by experimenting with drugs."
- "I forgive myself for my hatred toward my husband who was innocent of the crimes which were really the crimes of my father."
- "I forgive myself. I forgive."

The release this kind of forgiveness provides is indescribable to those who have never experienced it; it is like laying down the ten-pound load of pain strapped to your chest, which you have carried to bed, through each day, to work, into all your relationships. You put it down, truly lay it aside, when you forgive yourself. Then you can rejoin the dance of life.

Accepting Ourselves

I am still searching for an acceptable answer to the questions: "Why? Why me? What is it about me that seems to elicit abusive treatment from men?" I can believe that at this point there may be characteristics in my personality that encourage an abusive relationship. But I cannot and will not believe that at the age of ten I elicited this type of behavior.

I was abused sexually as a child from about ages seven to fifteen. . . . I heard someone say something about how a person stops growing emotionally when this happens. I think that happened to me because I have found that I am an emotional cripple. Emotionally, I am still seven years old.

For some time now I've been asking the Lord to show me why I am such a low achiever. I know it's because I set my standards very low, but why do I do that? I know I can achieve, but it seems like I don't want to, . . . or [feel I] shouldn't.

I was a victim of sexual abuse. I have very low self-esteem. It took me a long, long time to figure out that I was worth something.

Feelings of despair and hopelessness overwhelm me, and I think people can see how dirty I really feel.

Clearly the survivor of child sexual abuse needs to think differently about herself if she is to really move into new life with confidence. The circumstances of her past have programmed her to feel dirty, worthless, and unlovable. Her response to these feelings may take many extremes: over- or under-achievement, promiscuity or asceticism, hiding herself in unattractive clothing or obesity, or flaunting herself sexually.

The balancing gyroscope at the center of an abuse victim's being that should help her establish and maintain her identity as a person and a woman has been knocked off center. She stands in a circle and turns and turns and turns; when she stops, she can't find her balance but gropes and weaves and stumbles. For the abuse survivor, this dizzy confusion may continue in one form or another for the rest of her life.

Her guilt, real or false, her damaged inner self-conception, all present her with a negative image which she actually reinforces by refusing to accept positive information about herself and by virtually collecting data to verify her negative hypothesis about her own worth.

Rebuilding self-image that has been shattered is an arduous journey in learning to: (1) refuse the effects of the past; (2) nurture and even parent oneself in the present; and (3) achieve in ways that will provide esteem milestones for the future. This is no insignificant task.

The abuse survivor has learned to believe lies about herself. She has often swallowed them whole. She is like a beautiful handwoven basket filled with slips of paper on which are written only negative comments like: "You're a dirty slut." "You can't do anything right." "You're worn and can never be mended." "You're evil." "You're ugly." "No one loves you." "You can't love anyone." "Why don't you just get rid of yourself? Everyone would be better off without you." These negatives keep whispering from her past and she complicates her healing by negating herself. It's as though without realizing it, she sits down and writes out additional negative messages that she crams into the basket of her self-concept.

Some of these messages have actually been spoken by the significant people in her childhood. She is going to have to go back and ascertain who said what and then begin combating those inner memory tapes rather than reinforcing them.

Lack of positive verbal approval in a child's past leaves any one of us vulnerable; the parent who could never say anything good, or who always held up an unachievable goal, leaves us prone to a failure complex, workaholism, fears of success, deprivation neuroses, and also leaves us unnurtured and extremely vulnerable. When this vacuum is complicated by a sexual abuse incident, but particularly by long involvement in incestuous sex, the task of healing is enormous.

Learning to Be Your Own Parent

One thing we can do for ourselves is begin to be a parent to the child within us. Your whole past lives within your memory as though it happened yesterday. Though you may have hidden away the incidents, or you may have dealt with them to the best of your ability, the child of your past, the young self you once were, often acts up in surprising ways in your present.

We often ask women to find that child within, to find her at a moment of pain, to describe what she looks like, how old she is, how she is acting. Then we ask, "Now, what does she need?"

"She is crying," someone will say. "She is seven (or eleven or fifteen). She is feeling alone and frightened. She needs someone to love her. She needs someone to tell her not to be afraid. She needs someone to tell her how pretty her new dress is and how well she jumps rope."

Once this kind of contact is made, the adult self can often begin to affirm, to nurture, and to comfort the child self. You simply find the inner child of the past and do for it what your parents were unable to do for you. In this sense, you can become your own mother. You can embrace and protect the child in your imagination. You can react in horror at the abuse. You can say, "It was not your fault. You did not cause this. You are not guilty."

Very often the therapist becomes a surrogate emotional parent during certain periods of therapeutic work. A pastor becomes a father substitute; a friend becomes a nurturing mother, who cares, who is present, who says to us the words we have never heard but need so badly. The temptation in these relationships is to fixate on them because of past deprivation and to want to cling, to own, to hold. Skilled professionals will try to prevent this transference from getting stuck in the negative fashion; and those who are needy must teach themselves to recognize the relationships for what they are—gifts given for healing times rather than permanent relational institutions.

Once the survivor of abuse begins to develop facility with Scripture, with prayer, and with knowing and experiencing who God really is, vast strides are made toward the healing of the broken self-image.

At this point, the "listening prayer" discussed earlier in chapter 7 becomes a vital tool in differentiating between the negative image falsehoods of the past and the substitution of those lies with positive truths. We read Scripture, we work through Christ-centered meditation, we journal our prayers, and then we say, "Lord, what do you have to say to me today?" and we listen. Through the inner voice of his Holy Spirit, God often speaks powerfully to us regarding our damaged self-image.

One woman told us of her experience, "I'm from an abused past and I heard the Lord say to me, 'You are my beloved.' Oh, I know he loves everyone best, but when I heard those words, I felt as if he loved me best, loved me in a special way and I had never, in my whole life, felt that way." The miracle of this wonderful heavenly Father-God is that he has the ability to love each one of his children best! Such inner communications begin to heal the cracks of the shattered self.

Soaking in Self-Affirmation

Another step toward healing that survivors can take is to get in touch with their tenacious negative thought patterns. Sit down one day and write out all the negative things that you think about yourself. Then one by one, take them to the Lord in prayer and say, *Is this true? Is this true? Is this true?* Then listen to what God speaks to your heart.

Catch the thoughts, *I can't stand myself. No one likes me.* Challenge them with truth: "Some days I can't stand myself, but more and more I like what I am discovering. And furthermore, I do have friends. I will not believe this." This self-correction is hard work, because the habit of negation has been insidious and lengthy. Often we have become so used to it we don't realize we're doing it.

Make it a new habit to tell yourself something good about yourself every day.

You might want to create a self-affirmation list. Take a clean sheet of paper, write your whole name, and then list the positive things that you can honestly say about yourself. Number them and keep going while ideas come. Even if you can only come up with one good thing that you know about yourself, write it down. Reject, absolutely reject, any denial. Don't cross anything out. And don't write down anything negative. Deliberately hunt for items to add to this list. Your running total may look something like this:

Mary Sue Smith
1. I am kind, especially to small or hurt things.
2. I have a green thumb and help things grow.
3. I am courteous.
4. I have a nice nose.
5. I learn quickly.

Get a friend to help you. Ask: "What are some of the things you like about me? I need to add them to my self-affirmation list." Specific things from one's husband can help enormously as well. You need to know that he loves to hear you laugh, that you make home a place of refuge, that he is intrigued by your ideas in conversations with friends—whatever. Take it all and add it to the list.

You must not add mental disqualifiers to these comments. Just soak in the good stuff; let it sink in deep to the damaged self; repeat their words over and over, "Did you hear that, Mary Sue? Fred said he doesn't know another woman who could have handled that crisis with the children the way you handled it. He said he was proud of you." In essence you are writing and slipping these pieces of paper affirmations into your self-image basket.

Especially if you have grown up in an atmosphere that has denied you good feelings about yourself, or where you have been demeaned by word or by action, you need to build yourself up through such honest self-assessment and affirm yourself through positive feedback. When someone commends you for a job well done, don't pass it off in your mind as, *Oh, she just says that because she's nice.* You need that affirmation. When a child says, "Mommy, I love you. You're beautiful," it's true! Believe it. Reach out and accept the daisies that are being handed to you. Listen, believe it, tuck it in close to your heart. It is God speaking to you through the honest commendation of others.

Now increase your abilities. Try one new thing you have

never done before. Rent a car and travel somewhere; explore that unknown new place. Have friends over some afternoon for an old-fashioned English tea. Take up tennis or jogging. Write an article on an idea you have always wanted to explore and explain to others. Volunteer to be part of the office staff for a local political campaign. Plant an herb garden. Join a discussion group. Take a job in an area of work that interests you.

Each new adventure, each new ability we develop, gives us self-confidence, a feeling of accomplishment. These activities not only help us shake off our dark expressions but also give us assurances for the future. We are building tomorrow's self-esteem by the inner journey and the achievements of today.

Something You Can Do Right Now

Here is a practical, workable plan for redeveloping your thinking about yourself by bringing it into line with God's evaluation of you. Write each of the key Scriptures that follow on a piece of paper and tape each one up in turn on your most-used mirror for several weeks, so that when you look at your reflection, you will also see reflected back to you *how God sees you.*

When one verse has saturated your mind so that you can quote it, put up another. Over a period of time, you will gradually grow a new view of yourself—one not based on how others react to you, but one based on the eternal truth of what God has said about how he relates to you as one of his creatures. Ultimately, the worth of each of us resides not just in ourselves but beyond ourselves—in God's estimate of us. Even when we feel "down on ourselves," this does not negate our real and great value.

1. *We are valued by right of creation:* Throughout Scripture, God makes it clear that he values people above all his other creations; that, having made man in his image, he loves and goes on loving all of his human sons and daughters. Meditate on and make these words your own: "It is he who has made us and we are his; we are his people, the sheep of his pasture" (Psalm 100:3). Made in God's image, made for his joy and for fellowship with him, we belong to God by right of creation, and he loves us with the special love of the Creator for those he has designed.

2. *We are valued by right of redemption:* The fact that God loves us because he has made us takes on even larger implications when we see the meaning of the cross of our Lord Jesus Christ. For not only are we valued as creatures created by and for a king, our double value is demonstrated by the self-offering of Jesus Christ, "For Christ died for sins

Affirmation is the rightful inheritance of every child. You deserve this after all you have suffered, after the self-doubt with which you have battled. This is what Scripture calls "edifying" oneself. It is a Christian activity. Do it as much as possible.

The China Cup Can Be Made New

The abuse survivor may well feel like a lovely china teacup that has become chipped and broken, the imprint blurred, the handle lost. Badly patched, it has been stuck in the back of the cupboard. It needs the touch of a master craftsman—a craftsman like Otto. An immigrant from the old world, Otto's language was thickly accented, his shop small and cluttered.

---

once for all, . . . to bring you to God" (1 Peter 3:18). Our low self-esteem may be exactly proportionate to our limited understanding of what God has said about us in Christ.

Words to think about and remember: "This is how God showed his love among us: He sent his one and only Son into the world that we might live through him" (1 John 4:9).

How much God values each of us can be seen most clearly in the price he was willing to pay to "buy us back" from the "dominion of darkness." As Paul says it in Romans, "Where sin increased, grace increased all the more" (Romans 5:20). Throughout Scripture this theme resonates, "But God demonstrates his own love for us in this: While we were still sinners, Christ died for us" (Romans 5:8). The cost of our redemption is a guarantee of God's incredible love. God does not love us because we try hard—because we are good Christians—but because he made us for himself and found it worthwhile to buy us back from Satan and his dark kingdom.

3. *We are valued because of the Beloved's acceptance:* Paul takes great pains to teach, again and again, that we are accepted with God not because of our degree of goodness, but because of the perfect and wholly acceptable sacrifice of Christ. When we accept that sacrifice made on our behalf, we are fully identified with the Perfect One. These are big concepts. Because we are seen as part of this perfect Christ, God, who transcends time and process, already sees all what we will one day, in eternity, become.

More words to soak into your thinking: "Dear friends, now we are children of God, and what we will be has not yet been made known. But we know that when he appears, we shall be like him, for we shall see him as he is" (1 John 3:2).

But he could repair anything: the ornate molding that fell from old mirrors, the dimming paint of an original oil or broken china. He had the touch of a true artist, and when he had repaired something, it looked like new. He took great pride in his work of restoration.

God is such a Master Craftsman. With this difference: Because God is the Creator, God can make us truly new again.

Anyone who struggles with lack of self-esteem or a negative self-concept can begin to meditate on the Scriptures and other truths that are shared there. When you understand your position before God as taught in Scripture, your self-esteem healing begins to take on rapid forward mobility. These truths can become experiential in your day-to-day view of yourself. See the section marked "Something You Can Do Right Now" for a structured plan for rethinking your self-worth.

Here's what happens: We find our self-identity by losing ourselves in Christ's identity. Through this process, the tight knots of self-hatred and low self-esteem begin to be untied. We accept our worth as created persons, beautiful because of God's image in us. We accept the value—the expensive price tag attached to us by the death of the Lord Jesus Christ for us. And we say, "Father, I accept your evaluation of who I am."

Then, as we accept Christ's lordship, we allow his mind, his self, his love to begin forming within us. Ultimately, we renew our self-image not by focusing only on ourselves. That may be one of the real distinctives between a Christian path to healing and a secular one. We don't become aware of our self-worth merely by looking in, but rather by looking up.

10
Understanding the Abuser

Rita's Story

"Rita" is a winsome, self-possessed woman, with an attractive shyness about her. Now a counselor at a sexual assault center, she speaks in a quiet voice about her experience of sexual abuse and her ongoing emergence from the long shadow it has cast over her life.

The primary sexual abuser in my life was my stepfather. But before my stepfather, I was abused by probably ten or twelve other relatives: cousins, uncles—you name it—from a very early age. The earliest incident I can recall was when I was about five, sitting on an older uncle's knee while he played under my dress. That started it; then there was fondling, and later, with cousins much older than myself, full intercourse. It was always a part of my life.

When I was twelve my mother and father separated. Mom met another man, Gus, and we moved away from our hometown. Basically, it began with him paying a lot of attention to me, which was nice. I missed my dad a lot. But my stepfather's attentions kept getting more and more intense. Within a year, we had begun to have intercourse, and this went on for five years. I was twelve when it all started and seventeen when it came to a sudden stop.

I found it all very confusing. I wasn't sure why it was happening to me, and I couldn't figure out why other people couldn't see what was going on. An alcoholic, Gus was a real con artist and seemed to be able to keep my mother deceived. A lot of the time I felt almost like "the other woman"—like Gus was cheating on Mom and using me as the other woman.

I couldn't concentrate on school at all. I felt different from other kids and had no close friends. My mind was constantly preoccupied with what was happening at home. I would get up in the morning wondering if it was going to happen that night, wondering if there was any way I could avoid being at home alone with Gus. I remember that my highest mark in seventh grade was forty-five, and I dropped out of school near the end of ninth grade.

Then one day I asked to go to a birthday party for a young cousin I liked a lot. Gus didn't want me to go—he never let me go anywhere. This time I decided I was going anyway. When I got home from the party, all of my belongings—my bed, my dresser, my clothes, my bicycle, everything—were wrecked and thrown out in the middle of the street. After this rampage, Gus had slit his wrists. Mom had found him and had taken him to the hospital. Then she and I worked frantically to get everything back into the house so that people wouldn't know what was happening.

I had a problem, though. I couldn't find my school books. When I went to school the following Monday, I still didn't have my books. My teacher, who lived two houses down from ours, walked from his desk to mine, and in full view of the class, put my books on my desk. His action made me feel frightened and exposed; obviously, he knew what had happened. Maybe everyone did. I never went back to school.

Then I just stayed at home. Gus worked out of town. He'd be gone for a week and home for a week. Those weeks when he was gone were heaven for me. I spent a lot of time hanging around with a cousin about my age, going to the hockey games that were the main entertainment in our small town. That's when I began to realize that I had a certain kind of control over boys and men, and I started using it. I drank a lot, was very promiscuous, and just kind of hid the pain of my own deep confusion.

When Gus would come home, I would stay at home and be his good little girl. He never allowed me to have a boyfriend. I was never even allowed to look at a boy when he was around.

Everything finally came out when I met a young man—not really a boyfriend, but a brotherly kind of person who cared for me as a person and sensed that something was wrong. I had known him for a long time, but we had just begun to be special friends when, one night, we all arrived at the same dance. Mom was there, Gus was there, I was there, my friend was there. Partway through the evening, my friend came and asked me for a dance. Well, Gus was very protective of me. He just went crazy, fighting my friend right there on the dance floor.

But my friend wasn't going to give up. Now he knew something was seriously wrong in Gus's relationship to me. He waited until Gus was out of town, and then he came over to my place and asked me a lot of questions. Finally I told him what was happening. He got the whole story. He went straight to my mom and told her, and then I went to the doctor. I had ended up getting venereal disease from Gus; why I had never gotten pregnant is more than I'll ever understand. Certainly Gus never took any precautions.

My friend phoned Gus and told him that he knew and said, "Look. Don't come back here." Shortly after that, Gus killed himself. I struggled between feelings of guilt for having indirectly caused his death, and anger that he had gotten out of it so easily—leaving me to deal with all my pain.

"What kind of man would do a thing like that?" This question is one of the first that people ask when they finally bring themselves to acknowledge the horror of child sexual abuse. "What sort of man would betray a child's trust? What sort of man would harm his own daughter?"

Gus, the stepfather in Rita's story, is one kind of abuser, perhaps fitting quite closely the stereotype of the alcoholic, self-focused "con man." But there are other kinds. Listen to another victim's voice:

The man who molested me at age ten was—and is—a Christian, a family man, a pillar of the community and of the local church. I know that we are to pray both for the defiled and for the defiler. They are both victims of defilement. They both need ministry. And the defilement is deep. It is spiritual defilement as well as physical and mental.

Dr. Roland Summit, Associate Professor of Psychiatry at Harbor-UCLA Medical Center, identifies "traditional values" as characteristic of incestuous fathers:

The most typical incest offender is seen by his children as rigid, stuffy, and old-fashioned. He is likely to place a high value on the obedience of children and the subordination of women.

He may be sexually inhibited . . . and tends to project onto contemporary teenagers a rampant sexual preoccupation. . . . Ironically, his distrust of his own impulses, his fearful anticipation of his daughter's sexual awakening, his need to take control of her most intimate needs, his inability to empathize with the feelings of women and children, and his inability to acknowledge and communicate unmet sexual needs within a mature relationship, all combine to make him exploit the very relationship he is determined to protect.

Intrafamilial Child Sexual Abuse in the Christian Home

Two factors contribute to the prevalence of incest in Christian families. Many religious families have difficulty dealing openly with matters of sexuality and intimacy. And these families have a tendency to have authoritarian leaders—the men in these families believe they "own" their women.

Just because a person has psychological problems (including incest) doesn't necessarily invalidate his or her Christianity. Such problems are painful reminders that we are fallen creatures in a fallen world. Although a Christian profession of faith should contribute to emotional well-being, it certainly does not guarantee psychological perfection. The harsh reality of sin in our lives should cause us to be humble.

When we profess faith in Jesus, we bring our raw material with us, including all our maladaptive habits (poor communication skills, limited

Several other conservative traits have been found to correlate with incest. A strong belief in individualism and self-sufficiency promote isolation from a protective network of parental surrogates which might otherwise challenge the father's possessiveness. The isolation is increased if the family has judgmental religious beliefs . . . that emphasize the dangers in associating with people outside the chosen circle. . . .

It should be recognized without question that the relatively high proportion of traditionalist offenders still constitutes a tiny fraction of all conservative families. At the same time, we must be prepared to recognize that the decent, God-fearing, law-abiding pillar of the community is at least as likely to have committed incest as is the alcoholic swinger down the block.[1]

In *The Broken Taboo*, Blair and Rita Justice profile the kind of abuser who may well be active in the church. "Barbara's father exemplifies how people can compartmentalize their lives: He worked, he had friends, he went to church, he committed incest. Her dad became religious when she was five and began teaching Sunday school. Her mother also taught."[2] According to Heggen's research, religious families who hold rigid beliefs often teach their children a sense of "us and them"—of separation from the rest of the community. This may allow abuse in such homes to continue, because the child will

---

control of our impulses, obsessional thinking). Although our motives and aspirations change, at least partially, it takes time for them to become firmly established, which is what Christian growth is all about. That's why the church—as a vehicle of teaching, social support, and grace—is so necessary in helping us channel these new motives and aspirations into significant personality change.

My own counseling experience has made me aware that Christians have all types of problems—including being locked into incestuous relationships. Learning to hate the sin but love the sinner is especially difficult with incestuous abuse because of the devastating consequences for all the family members involved. But since we can never tell what raw material a person brings to his conversion, we should avoid the temptation to judge. Rather, we should ponder the best way to manifest God's grace to him or her.[4]

not feel free to seek help from outside of the family. Nor can she cry for help inside the family, since sexual matters are not to be discussed.[3]

In his article "Intrafamilial Child Sexual Abuse in the Christian Home," Richard Butman discusses some of the factors that may contribute to the prevalence of incest in Christian families and the attitudes Christians should take toward offenders (see inset below).

As we go on to look at the characteristic profile of the abuser, we dare not dissociate ourselves from him. For we will find that he is not only our neighbor. He is very often our brother.

Profile of the Non-Violent Abuser

What is the nature of the child abuser? Recognizing that such offenders are not all alike, can we nonetheless form a composite profile? Studies suggest some common characteristics of child sexual abusers, and it is worth our while to examine this information in order to achieve a clearer understanding of the dynamics of child sexual abuse and to find some answers to our horrified "why?" questions.

With such information, we can move toward actions that need to be taken:

- the personal act of forgiveness, which sets us free to care
- the family action of seeking counsel and legal redress
- the corporate action of church discipline where applicable
- the community action of prevention and rehabilitation

Our primary interest in this book is in child molesters (within or outside the family) rather than in child rapists or others interested in "cruelty relationships" with children. So we will look mainly at the characteristics of what are sometimes termed "non-dangerous" sex offenders—those who are basically nonviolent.

1. *Definition.* Researchers Nicholas Groth, William Hobson, and Thomas Gary offer this definition: A child molester is "a significantly older person whose conscious sexual interests and

overt sexual behaviors are directed either partially or exclusively towards prepubertal children."[5] Such people are often referred to by the term *pedophile,* which means "child-lover."

2. *Childhood Background.* While child molesters show clear signs of inadequate socio-sexual maturation, study results vary as to the extent of childhood trauma that non-dangerous child molesters themselves experienced.[6] According to a study by the Canadian Committee on Sexual Offenses Against Children, chaired by University of Toronto behavioral scientist Robin Badgley, 90 percent of the "non-dangerous" sexual offenders came from structurally stable families with numerous siblings. Three-fifths of the 90 percent were involved in an adult heterosexual relationship at the time they committed the child sexual offense. Only one in five was a stranger to the child at the time.[7]

But although some offenders may not have a history of childhood trauma, others have experienced childhood emotional deprivation that makes it difficult for them to form healthy adult relationships. This emotional scarring may stem from problems within the family or from lack of acceptance by peers during the growing-up years.

In a recent study, psychologists Sonia Dhawan and William Marshall found significant backgrounds of parental neglect, verbal abuse, and physical abuse among a small group of child molester inmates.[8] Similarly, a comparison of child molesters with men who were sexually abused in childhood but who were *not* accused of sexual abuse, revealed more verbal and physical abuse by parents in the child molester group.[9]

3. *Two Basic Types of Molesters.* Groth, Hobson, and Gary identify two basic types of sexual offenders against children on the basis of their levels of socio-sexual maturation.

(a) The Fixated Molester: This person demonstrates a compulsive and primary sexual preference for children. Male victims are primary targets. The persistent and compulsive behavior means that many children may be molested by one molester. One study showed that extrafamilial and intrafamilial pedophiles had an average of 90 victims and 2 victims, respectively—suggesting that extrafamilial molesters sexually abuse more children, while molesters who abuse children that are related to them abuse the same child more often.[10] Extra-familial abusers could often be described as "fixated"—tending to molest large numbers of children.

This fixation seems to be a result of inadequate resolution of maturation issues. The interest for sexual involvement with children is apparent from adolescence onward, with the molester showing little or no interest in sexual contact with peers.

(b) The Regressed Molester: This person successfully developed a primary sexual orientation to peers, but under some precipitating stress reverts to sexual contact with a child. Female children are primary targets, and the pedophilic sexual activity usually coexists with sexual involvement with a peer. This type of offender typically replaces a conflictual adult relationship with involvement with a child. In incestuous situations, the offender abandons his parental role and reverts to adolescent behavior patterns, behaving "not so much as a grown man . . . [but as] a maladroit adolescent attempting to win a young girl in his first love affair."[11] This offender copes with life stresses by regressing to an earlier stage of development.

4. *Behavior in Vulnerable Relationships.* Any relationship of authority or trust with children is liable to be abused by a pedophile. According to Dr. Summit, "Stepfathers are five times more likely to molest a child in their care than natural fathers. Live-in boyfriends and transient suitors [of the mother] are also more predatory, on the average, than the natural father."[12] We've all read news stories of foster parents, Boy-Scout leaders, reform school directors, security guards, school teachers—as well as parents—abusing the trust of children.

5. *Denial and Rationalization.* Many researchers point out the strong denial and rationalization mechanisms that are developed by people who flout the taboo against sexual activity with children. When confronted, "a suspect is both passionate and often very convincing in his protests of innocence," says Dr. Summit.[13] Some may actually have developed a denial system to the point of amnesia. Karin Meiselman comments on this denial/rationalization syndrome:

> The incestuous father generally tries to alleviate his guilt
> and anxiety by reiterating . . . the rationalizations that

he has been employing during the affair—his wife is frigid, his daughter is precociously developed and seductive, it is his duty to provide sex education, better him than another, and so forth. In trying to minimize the offense, he may insist that there was only "sex play" as opposed to intercourse. . . .

Some fathers react to the incest revelation with a strong denial of the offense. . . . When this reaction occurs, the daughter is portrayed in the vilest of terms. . . . If his wife wishes to continue their marriage, she joins him in repudiation of the daughter.[14]

6. *Marital Dissatisfaction.* Whether as part of the denial/rationalization process or as triggering stress, the abuser often expresses marital dissatisfaction. He may feel his wife is cold, domineering, or indifferent. Although this dissatisfaction may be rooted in the abuser's own immaturity in a sexual relationship, he is most likely to project his problems onto his wife and claim inadequacy on her part.

7. *Precipitating Stress.* As with other forms of child abuse, child sexual abuse is deeply rooted in the insecurity and low self-esteem of the adult and in his maladaptive ways of coping with life. And, as with other forms of child abuse, sexual abuse is often triggered by a particular stress (which the abuser may name as "the reason" in his self-justification and rationalization).

Wesley R. Monfalcone in *Coping with Abuse in the Family* names some of these triggering stress situations:

- financial crises, including unemployment or business reversals
- illness of a spouse, creating frustration and resentment
- a feeling of being trapped by the circumstances of life
- a nonsupportive or absent spouse
- alcohol and drug addiction[15]

Summit sees that "the man most often seeks sexual contact with a child when he is frustrated in his usual adult gratifications. He may be out of work, disabled, passed over for promotion, or rejected in an attempted affair."[16]

8. *Need for Power and Control.* The real issue in sexual molestation is more one of power and control than one of sexuality. With a child, the adult perpetrator feels he can be the undisputed dominant partner. Religious views that allow a man to feel he has the right to absolute control over his wife and daughters may be used as justification.

Shirley O'Brien investigates the emotional level of the perpetrator and states, "The adult perpetrator is trying to find an extension of himself with the victim. That is, he is seeking narcissistic autoeroticism. . . . Such an adult sees a relationship with a child as less threatening because in such a situation he does not feel inferior. He is in control."[17]

Most authorities agree that the child molester is arrested in his own psychological and emotional development. Louise Armstrong says, "The abusive father must have a sense of paternalistic prerogative in order to even begin to rationalize what he's doing. . . . Weak or authoritarian in nature, he must have a perception of his children as possessions, as objects. He must see his children as there to meet his needs—rather than the other way around."[18]

Profile of Dangerous Abusers

The majority of child molesters are not psychotic. Of course, there is a chilling minority who systematically prey on children with the intent to coerce, punish, torture, humiliate, and sometimes even maim and kill. These offenders, considered "dangerous" in the sense of being potentially violent, are very likely to have abuse backgrounds of their own. Along with experiences of neglect and abuse by parents, Dhawan and Marshall's study also found that 50 percent of the group of child sexual molesters they studied had been sexually abused as children.[19] Other statistics show even higher percentages of abusers who were themselves victims as children—significantly greater than the rates reported by nonoffenders. Freda Briggs and Russell Hawkins report that 93 percent of the eighty-four convicted child molesters they studied reported a history of childhood sexual abuse.[20]

Nicholas Groth notes in his book *Men Who Rape*, "The offender's adult crimes may be in part a repetition and acting out of a sexual offense he was subjected to as a child, a mal-adaptive effort to solve an unresolved early sexual trauma."[21] Some researchers suggest that child molesters were themselves sexually abused at the same age as the children to whom they are later attracted.[22] For instance, a male victim at the age of seven may later abuse boys that are around seven years old.

Some of the voices we heard echo these findings:

> *My husband was molested as a child. Then a few years ago he molested some little girls. He is emotionally abusive, and my son and I hate the way he behaves when he is angry. There has been so much hurt and damage, . . . and he still blames other people for things he did wrong.*

> *Yes, I too was abused as a child, but I had begun to believe my own rationalizations and would never admit even to myself that I was actually a molester.*

The Badgley report found that 98 percent of the potentially violent offenders came from broken homes. These offenders, in contrast to the nonviolent offenders, were rarely married, and most had previous criminal records. Three in four of the potentially violent offenders were strangers to the child at the time of the offense.[23]

Is There Any Justice?

A recent study of the outcomes of child sexual abuse cases found that many of the cases—around 40 percent—were dismissed. In 61 percent of the cases, the accused molesters did not go to prison. Most cases ended with guilty pleas instead of trials. When a defendant is convicted through this plea-bargaining process, his criminal record may not clearly show that he is a child molester. The prison sentence for those who plead guilty tends to be shorter as well.[24]

Charges are often dismissed because the child molester is judged to be nonviolent or a first offender, or because the family drops the charges. Usually, the only witness is a child whom prosecutors tend to regard as unreliable. The pedophile has often intentionally picked victims who would make the least credible witnesses in the event of detection.

The Badgley report noted, with irony, that when fathers committed against their own children the same offenses that "dangerous offenders" committed against strangers, they were rarely convicted as dangerous offenders.[25] Judges did not consider an in-family offense to be as dangerous as one committed against a stranger's child. Similarly, a study by the National Council of Jewish Women Center for the Child revealed that, in some areas, those perpetrators accused of molesting their own daughters are more likely to receive psychological treatment rather than prosecution.[26]

One hears, hauntingly, the prophetic judgment from the book of Isaiah: "So justice is driven back, and righteousness stands at a distance; truth has stumbled in the streets, honesty cannot enter. . . . The Lord looked and was displeased that there was no justice. He saw that there was no one, he was appalled that there was no one to intervene." (Isaiah 59:14-16)

Pornography and Child Sexual Abuse

More and more studies are linking pornography to early child sexual offenders. Psychologist William Marshall at Kingston Penitentiary and Queens University found that seven out of a group of eighteen rapists studied who used "consenting" pornography to instigate a sexual offense said that it provided a cue to elicit fantasies of forced sex. Similarly, ten of the eighteen who currently used "consenting" sex stimuli, used it to elicit rape fantasies. He writes, "In fact, the one rapist who reported using child pornography as an incitor actually raped a fifteen-year-old girl on that occasion. This again reveals the capacity of various forms of pornography to elicit favored fantasies that may lead to crime."[27]

In a later study, Marshall found that, out of a group of rapists and child sexual molesters, 33 percent used hard-core pornography before committing acts of sexual assault. Thirty-three percent of the rapists and—more strikingly—53 percent of the child molesters viewed pornography specifically to prepare for their assaults.[28] Similar results were found by the Los

Angeles Police Department, which studied 320 cases of extra-familial child sexual abuse over nine years. In 54.7 percent of these cases, the police recovered pornography.[29]

> *I remember the things my father forced me to do and the disgusting magazines and books he kept hidden away.*

———————

> *I would do anything to help stop the flood of pornography. My abuser regularly excited himself with it.*

Can Incestuous Fathers and Other Child Molesters Be Helped?

The attitude of much of the professional psychological community has been: once a pedophile, always a pedophile. Other experts state that help for the confirmed child molester, for the habitual incestuous father, is difficult, but no more difficult than that for the alcoholic—both are addicted to a habit beyond their control.

According to researcher Alexander Zaphiris, the best environment for healing is one in which professionals dealing with incestuous situations put aside their own revulsions and bring professional, diagnostic, and rehabilitative skills to their therapy; one in which the community (especially the law enforcement and the criminal justice systems) develops a nonpunitive and collaborative cooperation; one in which there is a unique treatment designed to include both the differences of individuals as well as the commonalities of incest; and one which includes a sufficient length of treatment (two to three years of weekly, one-hour sessions) to ensure a comprehensive and permanent outcome.[30]

Can abusers be helped? Yes, they can. With extensive therapy and a caring community, they *can* move toward wholeness. But in order to help them, we need to enter their worlds and listen to their stories, just as we have listened to their victims' stories. We need to put aside our own personal revulsions about the act of child sexual abuse and look at the abuser as a *person*, a fellow human being. Healing takes work, cooperation, and time, as "George's" story will show.

11
Portrait of an Abuser

"George's" Story

I'm thirty-five now. I grew up in a relatively well-balanced family, believe it or not, although I was always closer to my mother than my father. My father was very distant emotionally, quite a disciplinarian but not very able to show love or affection. As I grew up, I was not accepted by girls of my age. Children, though, accepted me and didn't comment on my face or scorn me, so I felt accepted by them.

I came to know the Lord in my late teens through a young people's group. I gave my life to the Lord—although there were some problems that I still held onto. I continued in fellowship with the church, becoming a deacon by the time I was thirty-one. In outward appearance, I was a very good Christian, but inwardly I knew I had some serious problems. I continued to experience attraction to little girls.

I married my wife when she had just turned eighteen. Our relationship was never really good. For my own part, I was playing roles; I appeared to be all together, but inside there were real problems and as time went on, the marriage broke down. At the time of our separation, my wife may have suspected something wrong in my relationship with our daughters, but she never really said anything. I don't think she knew that I had become incestuously involved with our daughters until I turned myself in to the police.

Our older daughter was about four or five when I started to caress her improperly. I knew what I was doing was wrong, and yet I reasoned that it wasn't really me doing it—it was the devil in me or whatever. I would say to myself, *Well, she doesn't mind it. She isn't saying anything. She isn't reacting, she isn't pulling away . . . so it's not that bad. Maybe she enjoys it.* And yet I never thought it was right. It is very hard to think about it now, but I did enjoy it. I would rationalize and say, "Well, God, forgive me. I know what I did was wrong, but it won't happen again." Until the next time.

I've learned in therapy that the offender does not view incest as a problem. Like other abuse offenders, I thought of the intimate caressing in which I was indulging as a solution to the big problems I had: the lack of communication and affection from my wife, for instance, and my own lack of self-confidence. Some people would use alcohol as a solution. Incest was mine.

My oldest daughter was the one I assaulted repeatedly. It is hard to think of it in those terms, but it is true. That is what I did. Although it was loving and gentle and caressing, it was still assault.

Then there were other children involved as well—family friends. One was four, and the other girls were between eight and ten years of age. One was the daughter of my best friend. I was trusted; I baby-sat the girls; I took care of them.

One fall day I did mention to my best friend the problems I was having with my own daughters. There had been a while in which I hadn't molested them, but suddenly within the span of two weekends I had again molested two girls. I knew I couldn't go on like that. It was way out of control and I couldn't seem to stop it. But my pride was in the way. How could I go and talk to somebody about that? They would view me as some horrible monster.

I asked the Lord, "Just what can I do to stop this?" I didn't know what to do.

After this there was a rapid chain of events. On Tuesday morning a couple of people phoned one of the elders and commented about my actions around young children—young girls—and the elder went and talked to my best friend to ask if he knew of any problem. My friend said, "Yes, there is a problem, but I don't know how advanced it is."

My friend went home that day and asked his daughter how she felt about me, and she said, "He touched me" and then cried for ten minutes. She told him what had happened—that I had fondled her inside her panties. He prayed about what to do for two days before he confronted me. He wasn't sure what to do. Then the Lord led a couple of people to talk to him about their role in child abuse cases. On Friday he came to me and said, "Look, either you get help or I will file a complaint." The elders contacted me Friday afternoon and asked to meet with me Saturday morning. At that point, my whole house of cards collapsed around me.

I was still feeling very sorry for myself. Every incest offender feels like a victim of everything else, like it is somebody else's fault. So on Saturday I went and talked to the elders and gave them a list of all the girls and told them in general terms what had happened. It was still hard to deal in detail with what I did. My daughters needed help, and I needed help because I knew that as they grew older, it would turn into intercourse.

The elders contacted Social Services, and I went over for an interview with them and told them about my daughters. I didn't tell them about the other girls. The elders contacted my wife (we had been separated for about a year and a half by that time) and told her what was going on.

At this point Social Services contacted the police and my minister did, too. I had no choice but to turn myself in. Then I was arrested and charged with sexual assault. I was allowed out on my own recognizance since they didn't feel I was a threat, but they did require a psychological assessment.

I was given a court date to go and face the charges, and two months later I pleaded guilty. During those months I had been continuing treatment with forensic assessment and an incest offenders group therapy program, which has really helped.

In therapy, they don't pull any punches; they tell it to you straight. The group members are there to work things out together and to say, "Look, you are giving us a snow job and you know it!" If you start lying, they know it, and they'll tell you. Psychologists and psychiatrists know the workings of the human mind and how the guards go up.

I know I need intensive treatment. You can't expect it to change in four months and then live happily ever after. It doesn't work like that. Incest doesn't go away by itself. You can pull the leaves off and cut it off at the stem, like staying away from children, from my daughters; but I can only do that for so long. Then, when we get back together, what is going to happen? I have to get treatment; there is no other way.

I was a pedophile. I still am. I have to understand that for the rest of my life I am an incest offender—like the alcoholic who has not taken the drink but still is an alcoholic.

I have seen the damage in my girls when they cry, when they feel very uptight about what they are discussing in counseling. The damage that I caused is enough to stop me, and yet given the possibility of being with a twelve-year-old under certain conditions—well, I just don't trust myself.

I have verbally, or through letters, told all the girls, "I am responsible, you are not." That is the terrible thing with incest—the guilt. Because the physical feelings are all there, a child does feel good but knows it is wrong. Thus there is a lot of confusion. So the father must take the responsibility and say and believe, "I did it, and it was me that did it, and you had nothing to do with it. It is wrong and I shouldn't have done that."

The church is still dealing with this situation and finds it very hard. The church at large has been negligent about this problem, thinking, "It could never happen here." At the request of the elders, I stood up and told the believers in the Communion service what was happening, that I was guilty of improperly touching girls.

The elders at one point got together with me and said, "You are not dealing with this. You say all the right things, but we don't see that anything has really changed. You are still manipulating; you are still trying to get people to accept you without change." They decided to withdraw church fellowship a week before I entered prison.

So on that Sunday I went to another church, and the minister preached on the difference between godly sorrow and human sorrow. Godly sorrow is repentance; human or worldly sorrow is manipulation. God really spoke to me through that man—the truth hit me between the eyes. That week in the incest group, we discussed my own view of what was going on, and the fact that I wasn't really dealing with my problem except on an intellectual level. They urged me, "Look, deal with it, and let us know what is really going on inside." I was afraid because I still had these feelings for children and I knew they were wrong. I had not assaulted any child since the time of the arrest a few months before, but the feelings were still there.

It was very painful because I was still trying to hide, and in that therapy session, before I was sentenced, I did a lot of work in the group and got a lot of things out. I worked through and started to deal with my feelings. It was a time of reckoning, a time of getting to know what is inside me, and a time of just being humbled before the Lord.

So much happened all at once—the breaking of fellowship at my church, the minister's sermon, the forcefulness of the therapy session, the sentencing when they read the charges before people in the courtroom and before the judge, the reading of what happened and how severe it was, the crashing of the prison doors, and the realization that I was here, in prison, because I broke the laws and sexually assaulted my own daughters.

God has used this to bring me to a point where I say, "Yes, I deserve to be here. I am the lowest of the low. I'm in with drug addicts and alcohol abusers; I'm in with people who are in for burglary and for assault—and yet even in this population, I am below them." This is not easy to take when pride has motivated so much of my life.

It has been very difficult for my church. I was very angry about the discipline at the time. Some people felt that it wasn't right to discipline me, yet it was very much what I needed. All the elders are good friends of mine; the church members are very good friends. I have known most of them for many years.

One thing that has to be understood about the incest offender—you can't let him off the hook, not for one instant.

The sex offender wants to take the easy road. It is harder to communicate with his wife than with his daughters. It is harder to communicate with an authority figure or a friend. So he turns to the easy route. But you can't feel sorry for him. He is the one who did it. He is the perpetrator. If they had let me off the hook, I would have continued. That is why the discipline has to be hard-line.

And it is very hard to be disciplined, to go through therapy, to go through a jail sentence. Yet that is what has to be done to start straightening out. I say that with a lot of conviction because I have been there.

In George's story, the reality of his crime was brought home to him by a church community that cared enough to discipline, by a brutally honest therapeutic exchange, and through sentencing and imprisonment. Without all of these, George might have gone to prison with his rationalizations intact, without coming to the point of saying, "I deserve to be here."

Drastic action does need to be taken. Removing the incestuous father from the home, beginning immediate intensive counseling for those "defiled" as well as the "defiler," openly confessing to the church community, disciplining, then giving firm, practical extensions of love—all these methods are intervening actions that separate the offender from his perverted intentions.

> *I am currently in jail awaiting sentencing because I had sexual intercourse with my daughter. I have confessed my sins to the church and have been formally separated from the church. I now know the Lord can and does change people who truly submit and confess their sins. There are many who have in Christian love stood by our sides and have given their time and means to help wherever they can.*

The Church's Helping Role
The Christian community, when educated to the complex magnitude of the problem of child sexual abuse, can function as

a healing unit to bring discipline, accountability, loving support, and a framework of true growth for the child sex
offender.

Historically, the church has been too timid in dealing with
the sexual offender, too quick to proffer forgiveness without
true repentance ("He said he was sorry, didn't he?"), too prone
to support the family as a unit rather than the individuals
within it. A family that fails to protect its own children is one
that needs radical dismantling and rebuilding. Hasty attempts
at reconciliation will probably only mean that the offense will
happen again. And again.

The church community must let the parents know that the
child is believed to be telling the truth, and that the family
has a serious problem that cannot be ignored. The family
should be told to get help and be guided in finding that help.
The parents need to know that the incestuous behavior is not
acceptable and must stop.[1]

What else needs to be done when abuse is suspected?
Juliann Whetsell-Mitchell suggests:

- talk to the child in a private place.
- remain calm and believe the child.
- call Children and Youth Services or Child Protective
  Services. (In many states and provinces it is now
  required by law that any known incident of child
  abuse, including sexual abuse, be reported to the
  police or Social Services.)
- reinforce verbally and behaviorally that the child
  acted appropriately.
- seek support and professional help for the parents.[2]

Remembering the strong denials and well-worked-out rationalizations of the child molester, church leaders must be wary
of "quick confessions" that relieve the offender of guilt but
do not mark a real about-face. True repentance is accompanied
by a desire to change, a willingness to face and accept justice,
and a readiness to make amends to the family and to enter
therapeutic counseling. To the child molester, Allender offers
these words: "The route to restoration is through brokenness.

Broken repentance will show in your willingness to submit yourself to the process of change through church discipline, counseling, interacting with other abusers, seeking wisdom and insight, and providing for the recuperative process of the victim."[3]

A genuine sorrow will result in a real acceptance of responsibility for both the crime committed and its long-term results in the life of the molested child or children. Even when the offender has been restored to communion, extreme wisdom must be exercised in restoring any ministry responsibilities in which temptation might be overpowering.

The church must become sensitive to the fact that *child molesters and incestuous fathers often are church members.* Once this reality is faced, the church must then become the community of healing. According to Heggen, when faced with child sexual abuse within the church, congregations must above all hold on to their belief in the possibility of new life in Christ—new life for the victim, for the perpetrator, and for their families.[4]

This belief in the possibility of real redemption and renewal within dysfunctional families should not, however, blind Christian leaders to the real complexity of the rebuilding, rehabilitative process. In the wish to get to happy endings, many leaders and pastoral counselors ignore the long-term repentance and accountability that must mark a genuine turning from any form of compulsive behaviors.

The Christian community must be concerned for the soul of the sufferer—the child as well as the adult perpetrator. It must intervene with spiritual authority, insist on truth, on confession, on an intensive therapeutic process. It must forgive and hear the forgiveness of the offender. It must love, support, supply physical means, and hold the offender accountable for seeking health. It must nurture the victim, find restoration of lost innocence through Christ, and pray for the healing of memories.

The church—what community on earth is equipped to do the job better?

12
The Mother of the Abused

Rita's Story

The hardest thing I had to deal with was my anger and resentment at my mother. How could she not have known what was going on?

I remember that at one point we were visiting relatives in another town, and I was sleeping with Gus and Mom (believe it or not). He was fondling me in the night, and she got up to go to the bathroom. Apparently she had seen what was happening, although she never said anything the whole weekend we were there. She never talked to me. She never talked to him. But when we got back home, she blew up.

At first she was really mad at him, but he talked her out of it. He conned her into believing that I had seduced him. "We really should do something with the child," I heard him say to her. "She's becoming a real problem."

I was thirteen at the time. I can recall sitting on the couch, hearing them talk, and thinking, *How can she believe all of this? How can she believe him over me?*

Gus came out of the bedroom where they had been talking, very nonchalantly. (I remember he was just wearing his shorts. He was always walking around in his shorts; he never wore pants around the house.) And he sat on the couch beside me, put his arm around me, and said, "I think maybe you should decide whether or not you are going to straighten out, or go to live with your father."

It just blew me away. My father is an alcoholic, and I didn't get along with his new wife. So I really couldn't go home to Dad. And although I didn't want to stay where I was, what other option did I really have?

So the relationship with Gus continued, although I think Mom chose to think it didn't. I never talked to my mother about it again, never trusted her again. Since she had taken his side once, I thought for sure that she would just blame me more for seducing him.

I knew nowhere outside my family to look for help, so I was effectively trapped in the situation. My mom used to escape to Bingo. She would go play Bingo to get away from Gus—and leave me with him. I would beg her to let me go, and he would talk her out of it. "She should stay home and do her homework," he would argue, or whatever. That was how he would get us alone.

Looking back, I realize she was what is called a collusive mother. She knew something was going on, but she couldn't have handled accepting it. Once I was in therapy, I was able to look at her situation a bit more objectively. I realize that our whole family is a very incestuous family. My mom got pregnant by being raped by her brother-in-law, for example. That same man went on to sexually abuse his own daughters for years and is now living with one by whom he has a child.

So I guess I understand now why she didn't react. She had her own past to deal with. But trying to build a relationship with her again has been the hardest task in my own recovery.

The Mother's Role
In a little antique shop, an old print hangs in the window. It shows two young girls holding hands, dressed in pinafores, walking through the ancient streets of a European city, stepping in the sunlight. In the lower lefthand corner of the print a dark, twisted man-monster crouches, observing their every move.

The picture, old-fashioned as it is, represents every woman's, every mother's deepest, most suppressed fear—that evil darkness may one day overtake the lighthearted innocence of the ones she loves most.

And yet, when the feared "monster" strikes, many mothers find themselves paralyzed—by their own crippling childhoods, perhaps; by societal expectations about building a "happy home"; even by biblical injunctions to submit to their husbands.

Mothers in incestuous situations may fall into one of three categories:

1. *Passive/collusive mothers* who, by remaining passive about an incest situation, give silent consent; many of them have experienced child sexual abuse themselves.

2. *Unaware/unbelieving mothers* who cannot/will not believe the child's report, thus doing great damage to the child's trust as well as recovery potential.

3. *Shocked/grieved mothers* who are prepared to act on behalf of the child. These mothers give the child the best chance to recover.[1]

Much has been written about the victim of early childhood sexual abuse; many studies are being conducted on the male abuser, but the *mother* (in cases of incest, referred to as the "non-offending spouse") often has to deal with an overwhelming array of emotions, a maelstrom that threatens to blow her world apart. The worst has happened. Now what is she to do?

> *My daughter was sexually abused as a child and has gone from one crisis situation to another, never really finding any happiness. . . . I cried and cried, and all I could think of was the molester and that he had left my child an emotional cripple.*

> *I am particularly discouraged by the total lack of any help or discussion of the effects of the revelation of sexual abuse on the mother of the abused, the wife of the abuser. I am both of these.*

I have not been able to find help for the mother of the victim.

The mother and the wife is also a victim. I have suffered tremendously in the last years.

The mother's role in cases of early child sexual abuse is pivotal—how she responds, how she handles conversations about the incident or incidents, and what type of comfort and support she gives to the victim, her child.

Parents must understand that a young child has barely enough language to describe sexual assault in a way that adults can understand, so parents must be careful listeners without slipping into paranoid suspicion. Sympathetic communication in a family should make talk on sexual topics easier.

But in all these incidents there seems to be such an inward moral taboo—somehow the heart knows that these hidden, secret actions are wrong—that open communication is not always easy, particularly between parent and child. One voice says,

Because we lived in the city while I grew up, my mother warned me about males who might attempt to take advantage of little girls. I was asked to reveal to her any incidents of this nature. But when the paperboy was verbally suggestive, I never dreamed of sharing this with my mother. I was too embarrassed because I sensed that she would be embarrassed.

How to Listen to Your Child

The parent must be very careful to pick up on the communication attempts of the child whose verbal ability is inadequate. A child might say, "I don't like Danny (a neighbor boy); he's dirty."

Instead of the usual parental moralizing, "Oh, no. Danny's not dirty. He's a nice boy," which immediately signals that the adult is not open to further conversation, it would be wiser in all cases to inquire, "That's interesting. Why do you think

Danny is dirty?" Then hold your breath and listen.

If the child says, "Danny pulled down Sandy's jeans," it is time to proceed with caution. Often a child will test parental waters of reaction by revealing incidents about *other* children (the same way a fearful adult will tell a counselor about the problem of a "friend"). "That's not very nice is it? Did he do anything else to Sandy?" It is to be hoped that the child, in this moment of tenuous revelation, will feel that she has a wise parental confidante, that she is loved, that nothing she has to say is so traumatic it cannot be handled by a calm, confident authority.

Very often parents don't pick up on the cues because the shadow hanging in their own subconscious mind is so terrifying. One must keep in mind that the victim of sexual abuse is most often pressured into secrecy about the sexual activity by the abuser, leaving the child feeling helpless and guilty, with no place to turn for help and no acceptable way out.

There are very real physical indicators to look for:

- A child's clothing appears stained, torn, or bloody.
- A child reports pain, itching, bruises, or bleeding in the genital area.
- The child is diagnosed as having a sexually transmitted disease of eyes, mouth, genitalia, and/or anus, or is found to be pregnant.
- The child experiences nightmares, bed-wetting, or changes in sleep patterns.

Some behavior indicators might be:

- Abrupt changes in behavior—sudden periods of quiet or depression, unusual belligerence or disobedience—any extremes that are not usual to the child's personality.
- Teachers pointing out unusual behavior patterns that have not been noticed at home. Children often "act out" a problem on the playground or in the classroom.
- An air of secrecy, hiding sexual material or being vague about whereabouts or activities.

- Using language or terms to describe the body, sex acts, or sexual deviations that are not appropriate to the child's age or experience.
- Obsessive talk about a person known or unknown to the family, or sudden, unreasonable intolerance of such a person.
- The unexplained appearance of gifts or material goods not given by members of the family.

What to Do with Your Anger

Without doubt, one of the most stressful moments is the moment when an adult learns that his or her child has been the victim of sexual molestation; but at this moment, no matter how overwhelming the feelings of the adult, it is the child who must have the primary consideration. The best reaction is to demonstrate a slow, cautious concern.

Expressed rage and anger may frighten the already frightened child, and such outbursts from the parent need to be qualified: "I'm sorry I upset you. I am very angry, but I am not angry with you. I'm angry at the person who did this to you." A victim of child sexual abuse often feels personally at fault, so the parent must be very careful not to cast blame with questions such as "Why weren't you more careful? How many times have I told you not to play in the park after dinner?" etc.

Ten Messages for the Child

In the book *We Can! Combat Child Sexual Abuse,* Shirley O'Brien suggests ten important messages that must be conveyed to the child, either verbally or nonverbally.[2] These are:

1. "It's O.K. to tell me about it."
2. "I believe you."
3. "You are safe with me."
4. "I am determined to put a stop to this."
5. "It's O.K. to feel . . . "
6. "It was not your fault."
7. "Some people take advantage of children."
8. "I'm sorry about what happened."
9. "I will help you."
10. "I care about you."

If you sense that a child has made a tentative confession, such as "he played with me," some gentle encouragers to further revelation might be: "Can you tell me what happened? How did he play with (touch, hold) you? Take as much time as you want. Use your own words. Mommy (Daddy) will not be mad at you. I want to help you, and I love you."

A question often asked is whether or not the child victim of sexual abuse needs counseling. It often depends on the intensity of the event, the damage, and what kind of trauma the child has experienced. Certainly, if unsettling symptoms persist several months to half a year after the disclosure, then the wise parent should seek professional guidance. Some symptoms might be lingering bad dreams, unusual fearfulness, bed-wetting, or any continuing drastic change in behavior patterns.

It is often the parents, rather than the child, who may benefit most by discussing their initial feelings and reactions with a trusted counselor. The parent is the child's safest harbor. And with perceptive guidance from a professional, the parent is often the one who can give the comfort, security, affection, and healing that the child needs.

Many psychotherapists suggest that even if all seems well, it is advisable for a girl raped in childhood to have the benefit of preventative therapy as she reaches adolescence. The teen years are fraught with emotional and psychological turmoil, and a therapeutic checkup at this time might ensure that these years will not be further complicated by the residual effects of an early traumatic sexual experience. This would be the time to ascertain whether effects remain and to help assure the teen that her future emotional and sexual relationships can be healthy and happy.

Incest—Its Effect on the Mother

The discovery of child molestation is a traumatic and stressful event in any family, but the discovery of incest is like stepping into the viper's nest.

The mother who has discovered that the abuser is her own husband, or the child's father or stepfather, finds her role excruciatingly complicated. There is a triad that begs her concern—her child, the victim; her husband, the betrayer; herself, the betrayed—not to mention the rest of the family. One casual glance at the damaging potentials can convince the most uninvolved bystander that the hazards are explosive enough to blow the family apart.

Second only to the victim herself, the mother of the victim suffers the most profound emotional upheaval. Her immediate reaction is one of shock. She may feel a gamut of emotions in rapid succession: repulsion so strong that it ventures on actual physical nausea; confusion as she is torn between a whirlwind of polar loyalties (to her child, to her husband whom she still loves); jealousy which is soon supplanted by a deep, bedrock conviction of failure; betrayal by both her husband and her daughter. All of this is further complicated by rage (if there is any emotional energy left for it); and always the nagging, continual feelings of guilt.

I was in shock; it was like a death finding out.

———————

After a year I have so much anger it's terrible. Please pray that she will make it through her adult years without a breakdown.

———————

I cannot tell you the years of worry and frustration I have endured since all that transpired. Even though I have forgiven, I suppose I'll never forget. My daughter continues to suffer.

———————

Something whispered inside me, He is molesting her, *but how can one think such a thing about one's own husband? The guilt I bear for not paying attention to my instincts is overwhelming.*

———————

It seems as though I can spot these men on the street,

office, anywhere I go. I have never been able to trust another man since then.

Oh, God, the guilt has been almost more than I can bear. I did not know.

And the mother experiences grief at the loss of her marital relationship. How can it ever be the same? How can she ever trust her husband again? Her security is shattered, as well as her hopes for the future. She is also faced with possible financial uncertainty if he is arrested or the marriage is dissolved.

No woman under any other stress—death, severe illness—needs more support.

Her situation may be further complicated by a husband who denies his involvement, who blames the incident(s) on the "seductive" child. Consequently she is forced to choose between her spouse and her child; and if the marital relationship is already particularly unequal in power, if she is the unduly submissive/passive type of woman, or if the male is in any way abusive, she is faced with overwhelming emotional odds.

Researchers agree that at this moment, *the mother's support and belief in a child's revelation of incest are the most important elements in the child's recovery.*[3] With this knowledge, she may feel forced to jettison her marriage—a form of self-sacrifice terrible in its implications for her and the rest of her family.

Now she begins to cope with outside opinions. Questioners ask why she allowed it to happen, implying that she knew about the situation and simply ignored it. This is an opinion often shared by many of the victims themselves—"Mother is all-knowing. She knows when I lie and when I don't do my homework. How could she not know that Dad and I . . . " Others may insist, "If you had sexually satisfied your husband, he wouldn't have turned to your daughter."

Of course, sometimes the mother is maladjusted—all too often a victim of abuse or incest herself. In many incestuous families, she has become passive and, like Rita's mother, allows something to happen that is too big for her to handle. In these situations, there is often a mother/daughter role reversal with the adult becoming dependent upon the child or absenting herself because of work, emotional unresponsiveness, or illness. When this happens, the daughter functions as the wife-surrogate, child/mother to the mother/child.

This role reversal deprives the daughter of utterly necessary maternal nurturing that helps her form a healthy opinion of her own female self. The sexual relationship with her father satisfies her underlying need for physical affection and closeness, putting her in a flip-flop power struggle; he has coerced and manipulated her, and now she can emotionally blackmail him. She is also provided with a means of expressing her unconscious wishes of revenge against a mother who has psychologically abandoned her.

In one study, incest survivors examined many years after the affair indicated that anger at the mother was a serious problem in adult life. Of the daughters studied, 40 percent continued to experience strong negative feelings toward their fathers, while the other 60 percent could be described as forgiving, although there were often problems with past resentments cropping up in the present. The opposite result was found with regard to the mothers—60 percent were definitely disliked by their daughters, while 40 percent were more positively regarded.[4]

Janet Liebman Jacobs adds that a majority of the female incest survivors in her study blamed their mothers for the abuse. The blame sometimes comes from the denial the mothers exhibit when they are told about the incest. In other instances, the daughters are convinced that their mothers were aware of the abuse—although they never directly told them about it. The survivors feel betrayed that their mothers did not act to rescue and protect them.[5]

An increasing number of observers, however, are beginning to find fault with the concept of the mother as a causative factor in incest. Some theorists feel this explanation blames mothers instead of blaming the abusive fathers and a society that permits abuse.[6] Sometimes mother negligence is involved; sometimes there is a passivity that amounts to collusion. But in many cases, this is not so. Louise Armstrong says:

> I hope that great care and thought is given to telling the
> mothers the ways in which what happened was not their
> fault. All wives and mothers have received a binding
> double message. As wives, we have been told our pri-
> mary responsibility is to support our husband. To stick
> with him, to endorse his behavior, his decisions, through
> thick and thin. As mothers, we have been told our pri-
> mary responsibility is to support our children. Can we
> blame women who, in crisis, are unable to decode this
> double message?[7]

Help for the Mother

What needs to be done for the mother? The Nanaimo Rape
Assault Center lists several helps for mothers in its book *Realities of Child Sexual Abuse:*

1. The mother of an incest victim, especially at the time of
disclosure, is suffering a major life trauma and will need massive support.

2. The mother may have requested help in the past and may
need help in counteracting negative messages of blame or disbelief.

3. The mother's need for support, reinforcement, and acceptance will continue for a lengthy period as she strives to
deal with the emotional damage done to her and to her child.

4. The mother may require assistance with such everyday
concerns as food and housing for herself and her children.

5. The mother may find herself in interaction with the legal,
criminal justice, and human resources systems. She needs information about their procedures and emotional support when
dealing with them.

6. The mother's traditional support systems may be disrupted as friends and family react in various ways to her situation. She may be under intense pressure from these people
to refrain from taking any action against the offender. She
needs support in the decisions she makes, whatever they may
be.

7. The mother may fear for her emotional stability as she

undergoes the usual responses to her disrupted life. She needs reassurance that her reactions are expected and manageable.

8. The mother needs constant reiteration of these messages: "I believe you." "You are not the offender." "Your emotions are acceptable." "You and your child can recover."[8]

Every incestuous family should undergo thorough therapeutic counseling of some kind. Something has gone desperately wrong somewhere in their family. The pattern of abuse must be broken.

The victims—the child and the mother—both need help to recover. If at all possible, the family needs to have a chance to mend and find health. The perpetrator must be held accountable for his actions, be forced to face his own devious immaturity, and then be firmly led to a path of repentance and potential restoration.

It takes skilled professionals to juggle so many precariously balanced pieces, but our voices speak of hope.

I know God is working to heal the scars in [my daughter's] heart and mind. God still performs miracles; he did a miracle in our home. Praise the Lord forever.

13
Renewing Relationships

Rita's Story

I met my husband, Dave, before I left home. I was eighteen years old and doing nothing, going nowhere. We got to know each other and just kind of moved in together, marrying later on.

Well, we had a son, and things got really rough. Dave was from an alcoholic home; I was from an alcoholic home. We were heading into a very sick relationship. He needed somebody and I needed somebody. The problem was, I needed somebody strong and he needed somebody strong—and neither of us was strong.

Sex was a real problem for us. I had a very hard time with it. In fact, I still do. I have a hard time giving myself fully. Even just going to bed and going to sleep can be hard for me. I still find myself listening for those hated footsteps of my stepfather down the hall. For a long time, the only way I could get to sleep was to fantasize about a Prince Charming who would come and hold me and that was all. Just hold me, never ever want sex. And with that fantasy, I would finally get to sleep.

Flashbacks would constantly interrupt our lovemaking. I would have my eyes closed, and when I would open them I would see Gus's face instead of Dave's. And suddenly I would push Dave away, unable to respond.

For me, making love was just a duty, something I felt I was supposed to do. I myself felt nothing. Absolutely nothing. At the same time, I wanted sex, because it was the only way in which I understood love to be expressed. So I got very good at pretending. Since therapy, I am able to be more honest and we are working things out. For example, if a flashback comes, I say, "I need some time; I'm having a problem." My husband is getting more and more understanding.

Another problem we faced was Dave's tendency to violence. He never hurt me, but he could really damage furniture. While he was growing up, his father was a very violent alcoholic—the sort of man who used to shoot holes in the wall and shoot at his wife. The kids used to have to hide in the bush when their dad came home drunk. All of that affected Dave, of course.

While we were struggling with our relationship, my oldest brother met the Lord. An alcoholic and a drug addict, he was really delivered and began attending a Christian fellowship. My brother and I have always been good friends, and he just kept talking to me and talking and talking and talking—and finally I started to go with him.

I can remember sitting with him in church one Sunday night when an invitation was being given for people to come forward to make a commitment of their lives to Jesus Christ. As I thought, *Not me. I'm not going up there. No way am I going up there,* it just seemed as if the Lord himself picked me up and took me up there. I found myself at the front—and that's when I prayed and invited Jesus into my life.

After I found the Lord—or should I say, after the Lord found me—Dave started to see little changes in me as he had seen big changes in my brother. At about the same time, his father also had a spiritual awakening, and it seemed like all around us there were people coming to the Lord.

Dave has made a commitment to Christ, but he still has a lot of problems. He is a depressive person with very little sense of self-worth. He has only a sixth-grade education, and he's ashamed and afraid to talk with anybody—even a counselor. He still has a bad temper. At the snap of a finger, he can explode into a violent rage. But he is working on it. He even gets up every morning and goes to the church for prayer services. He is a lot more open in sharing with me now, and the more we talk, the better it gets.

Of course, we still have lots of problems to work out. But I know if it weren't for the Lord, we wouldn't be together at all.

One psychiatrist reports, "Typically, patients with great difficulty in forming lasting relationships often have abuse backgrounds. A standard pattern is that of forming very intense relationships which they are then unable to sustain. Having set themselves up for rejection, they spend a lot of time experiencing the pain of rejection."[1]

Difficulty in relationships is often a symptom of a background of abuse, but the symptoms form differing patterns. One person may seem socially poised, but keep people distant; their poised control raises a subtle sign reading: *Private Territory/Do Not Enter.* Others may be withdrawn, even antisocial. But both are equally threatened by the intimacy of real friendship.

Some may be able to think of human relationships only in sexual terms. They may become extremely possessive in relationships, developing a leechlike obsession with the other person that eventually drives the sought-for friend away. Or they may be unable to make any lasting attachments because of deep insecurity.

> *I want so much to be a good wife and mother, . . . but I find myself off-balance a lot of the time.*

> *When my husband stands over me (before we have sex), I feel terrified, out of control, like I'm losing myself.*

> *I have really never wanted to let anyone get to know me. I've always wondered, "If they knew, what would they think?"*

New Parental Models Are Needed

In addition, in incestuous families where the father has been the perpetrator and the mother has been passive/collusive, emotionally distant, or has chosen to disbelieve or blame the child, the whole modeling system by which a child forms her ideas of sex roles and adult behavior is disrupted. The victim finds great difficulty in forming healthy male and female relationships. Again, an effort-filled process of reconstruction is necessary.

Early child sexual abuse distorts the ability to perceive men as possible friends or as accessible adults worthy of trust. The "flirt/freeze" mentality described by many of the voices we've heard intervenes. Men are viewed primarily in their sexual role and are believed to be "all out for the same thing." Some women have developed a first-strike style in human relationships, a "get-them-before-they-get-me" approach. The men in their lives must deal with a come-hither, flirtatious sexual invitation (issued either because of true desire, or unconscious patterned behavior), or a barely suppressed irrational antagonism.

Both styles are, of course, unhealthy, immature social realizations. The abuse survivor's situation is complicated when her flirt/freeze behavior is responded to with the male's own particular brand of anti-feminism, his own private source of hatred, his stereotypic idea system, his own bedrock belief that women are simply sexual objects to satisfy his own physical needs.

New Testament Standards for Relationships

Can there be any greater breakthrough in male/female relationships than the New Testament writings of the apostle Paul? St. Paul, often wrongly labeled a male chauvinist, proclaimed: "There is neither Jew nor Greek, there is neither slave nor free, there is neither male nor female; for you are all one in Christ Jesus" (Galatians 3:28, RSV).

Paul applies this scriptural truth even more specifically in his instructions to Timothy, where he sets the personal standards of behavior that a young leader should model in Christian community relationships between the sexes: "Do not rebuke an older man but exhort him as you would a father; treat younger men like brothers, older women like mothers, younger women like sisters, in all purity" (1 Timothy 5:1-2, RSV).

Paul's standard for Christian community is the standard of the healthy family.

What a relief it is to learn how to relate to others without a sexual agenda! While a wise and natural caution is in order in all male/female relationships because of the power of our sexuality to pull relationships toward physical expression, we still maintain a firm belief that learning to view men not as potential lovers but as potential brothers is the first step to freedom. (Some women involved in past sexual relationships with their brothers will have to make the extra effort of putting aside the old pain, of relating to men along the lines of what a brother should be.)

One married male friend admitted honestly to me, "There are many women I am attracted to sexually, but once I have gotten to know them, the sexual attraction ceases, and we are able to develop mature, Christian male/female relationships." We need to understand that sexual attraction often diminishes as we deny its preemptive position and prayerfully push forward to relate together as humans before God, all children in God's family.

Interestingly enough, when parents have been what parents should be, giving the nurture, the love, the affection, the affirmation that is every child's due, the ability to establish healthy nonsexualized brother/sister relationships is enhanced in the adult years.

In fact, many child psychologists are discovering that it is the loving father who helps both his male and female children feel good about their own sexuality. The most wonderful gift a father can give to a child is fond, affirmative, positive affection. If he says to his daughter, "You are so beautiful. I'm so proud that you're my little girl"; if he clearly enjoys her company, shows interest in her interests; if he hugs and cuddles and wrestles; if he verbally encourages her, he is filling the love-well from which she will draw in her adult years in order to be able to relate as a whole person, not as a needy object.

The tragedy in all this discussion of sexual abuse would be for healthy fathers to become overly scrupulous and to cease loving their children in naturally exuberant, healthy ways. We need better fathers in the church, fathers who parent their own children well and also take a few others under their umbrella of cherished protection.

It may be more difficult for some people than for others to achieve the goal of nonsexualized brother/sister relationships. But it is nonetheless a goal toward which we can strive together. The church must constantly evaluate the ways in which it is teaching and exemplifying such relationships.

Unfortunately, much biblical exposition has emphasized a hierarchical male/female structure. This may, unintentionally, make it difficult for the abuse survivor to feel accepted, welcome, and safe within the caring, nonexploitive community that the church must be. Renewed efforts are needed to open doors into this sheltered society that is especially able to commit itself to the healing and growth of the wounded within it.

Woman to Woman

Strangely enough, it is often the male/female sexual attraction that destroys our sister-to-sister relationships. The joy of strong friendships with other women has been celebrated recently by feminist writers who pointed out that the competition between women for male attention is what often prohibits healthy inter-female relationships.

Euripides once said, "Woman is woman's greatest ally." We need to work to understand one another, to bear one another's burdens, to do unto others what we would have others do unto us, to be hospitable to each other—all Christian concepts.

While working with female patients, Sigmund Freud claimed (in *Studies on Hysteria)* that child sexual trauma was the cause of every case of hysteria. Later he rejected this theory because of the astonishing fact that children laid blame on perverse acts by the father. Incest couldn't be that frequent, he reasoned, and thus developed his explanation of this phenomenon as being due to female "oedipal" fantasies toward fathers, which had no basis in reality.[2]

Later on, Alfred Kinsey's massive 1953 report on modern

sexuality never denied the reality of child sexual abuse, but Kinsey himself did as much as he could to minimize its importance. Some 80 percent of the women who had experienced a childhood sexual approach by an adult reported to the Kinsey investigative team that they had been frightened and upset by these incidents. Kinsey belittled these reactions. He hastened to assure the public that children should not be upset by these experiences. If they were, he reasoned, this was not the fault of the sexual aggressor, but of prudish parents and teachers who caused the child to become hysterical.[3]

In general, it was women who first listened seriously to women. Female professionals since 1970 have been largely responsible for exposing the prevalence of sexual abuse and bringing it to public attention. And once educated about the incredible reality of early child sexual abuse, church women show an enormous capacity to be supportive.

One woman undergoing therapy suddenly began to get in touch with her traumatic memory of past abuse. She went through several months with nights shattered by dreams as the memories of past events surfaced. A small group of church friends took turns sleeping in her house, comforting and loving her family through this agonizing period, sharing homemaking responsibilities, and supporting her husband until the worst was over. Her therapist termed this burden bearing "an ideal healing model."

The Church's Help

An article on child abuse in the *Sunday School Counselor* reiterates the importance of church involvement. Author Gene Smiley writes: "The church is ideally equipped to minister to families during times of extreme stress and emotional trauma. The acceptance, love, forgiveness, and support roles that are at the very heart of the church's message are exactly those required for proper remediation, healing and restoration of families who have been traumatized."[4]

Christ, in his compassion for both men and women, intended for us to form a new society, a kingdom society on earth that modeled the kingdom society of heaven, with little emphasis placed on sex roles but much emphasis on doing the work of God. The church has the potential for creating this harmonious society in small, spirit-empowered communities here on earth in several ways.

1. *True Peace—God's Peace.* For instance, for the abuse survivor, the sacramental use of touch encouraged by Scripture and practiced by many liturgical churches ("greet one another with a holy kiss," Romans 16:16) has great potential for healing, for nonthreatening physical impact. Imagine being embraced every Sunday, before every Eucharist, as men and women speak the words of Christ to each other: "Peace be unto you." To be touched, to be held, with no thought of sexuality intruding; to have the words spoken that lay to rest the war between the sexes and the alienation between humans—"Peace be unto you . . . God's peace"—can be incredible in its efficacy.

The bishop of a large Episcopalian diocese told of a time early in his ministry when he had been at odds with "an obnoxious curate." One day at Morning Prayer, they found that they were the only two in attendance. At a certain point in the service, the peace was passed. "As we embraced and spoke the peace, without words, our animosities were dissolved and from that day our hostilities were ended." Can this not be a means to ending the hostilities between brothers and sisters in Christ that we each bring from our uniquely damaged pasts?

2. *Communion—The United Family.* The movie *Places in the Heart* ends with a scene in a little country church where the congregation sings a hymn and partakes of Communion. Suddenly the heroine's dead husband is sitting there beside her, then the town racist beside the black man; then those who have been at enmity pass the cup and share the bread. In symbolic array, the filmmaker visually displays what happens to us every time we partake of this sacrament: we are brought into communion with Christ and with his body.

If you want your relationships restored, we encourage you to use the healing potential of these offices of the church. Before you partake of Communion, examine your heart: Whom do you still hate? Who still has the potential to wound you, either in real life or in memory? Take them to the altar in your mind (or invite them to sit beside you in the pew) and receive the elements with them, asking to be freed from their power, from the hatred, from the broken relationship. Pray for God's love to reach them at that moment in this unbroken communion with Christ.

3. *Ministering Christ.* The ministerial role, the priestly role, is also powerful. An ordained minister who understands that he/she ministers Christ can be an agent for healing redemption to the abused. A faithful priest *functioning* as a faithful priest can often shorten the therapeutic process. To make Communion available after therapy sessions in which the painful past has been invoked is an act of healing and pure compassion; we are nourished and reminded again of the risen Christ through the bread and the cup.

If your church doesn't have a service for healing, find one that does. Ask for those hands to touch you in the name of Christ, for the oil to mark your forehead in the name of Christ, for the circle of protection to form around you in the name of Christ. Listen to the prayers, spontaneous or ancient, that human voices pray, often speaking on behalf of Christ. Place yourself in God's circle by learning to renew your relationships in the family of God. (See Appendix C for suggested prayers and litanies.)

These healing tools are available to us, but unfortunately many nonliturgical, evangelical churches have little understanding of their potential. And the liturgical churches, with their weekly enactment of sacrament, have often lost sight of the sacramental meaning—that God can touch us through holy moments, holy acts, holy hands. We need to rediscover their supernatural potential in our churches today for the sake of this needy, broken world and the people in it.

A New Family

The body of Christ often gives us new mothers and new fathers. Paul writes about the familial responsibilities of the Christian community: "Bid the older women . . . to teach what is good, and so train the young women to love their husbands and children." (Titus 2:3-4, RSV). What a comfort for the survivor of abuse who is at a loss as to how to behave in human relationships! What potential for holy women to model what has been forfeited by the terrible past. The lonely one no longer has to go it alone. The victim does not have to be the victimizer. She can be taught to walk in a new way, freeing her children from the destructive patterns of her past.

In a courageous book titled *Out of Control! A Christian Parent's Victorious Struggle with Child Abuse,* the author shares how she struggled to overcome child battering with her own small child. She came to terms with her abusive anger partly through the women in a Bible study group, who prayed for her and gave her good parenting advice, and partly with the help of an older Christian woman on whom she could call when the home situation got rough.[5]

There is no reason why a local church cannot provide all of these forms of assistance for members of their congregation, not to mention reaching into the resources of the larger community. Study groups that develop a philosophy of Christian parenting should be a part of every church's training curriculum. Older men and women who have been successful parents should be available to answer questions and to guide. Parents also need to find a person who will hold them accountable, provide emergency assistance, arrange to take the children out of the home when intervention is necessary, and intercede in prayer. These friends can help abusive parents learn to deal with unhealthy behavior and inappropriate anger in an adult way so that their homes can become Christ-centered.

The parent with a background of abuse does not need to abuse her own children. The cycle of anger, terrorization, rejection, and trauma can be broken. The church can learn to listen and *keep confidentiality,* another priestlike capacity. Such a gift for the innocent survivor of a shame-filled past is welcome and comforting. As one woman said, "I'm not one to make friends easily. I select people who aren't gossipers, for those women can stone you to death."

Christ was the advocate of little children:

> "Whoever causes one of these little ones who believe in me to sin, it would be better for him to have a great millstone fastened round his neck and to be drowned in

the depth of the sea. . . . See that you do not despise one of these little ones; for I tell you that in heaven their angels always behold the face of my Father who is in heaven. . . . So it is not the will of my Father who is in heaven that one of these little ones should perish" (Matthew 18:6, 10, 14, RSV).

Jesus felt that way toward you when you were abused; he feels the same toward the child you are raising today. He is the same Christ who said, "Let the little children come unto me." He is the one who asked the men who harassed the woman who came to anoint his feet, "Leave her alone. Why are you bothering her?" (Mark 14:6). This Christ was familiar with abuse; he went through it himself. He was humiliated, stripped, and scourged, lifted up naked to die a brutal death. He knows what you have endured and what you are going through. He suffers with you.

But he also offers hope—hope that we can finally complete the journey toward healing. There is potential for the *renewal* of all relationships in the church; there is potential for the *healing* of relationships within the church.

> *My healing started when I told my husband-to-be that I wasn't a virgin and I told him why. His response sounds in my ears as loud now as then. He said, "If you were a harlot, which you weren't, and the Lord had said, 'She's the one,' you would have been as pure as driven snow." Those were wonderful healing words, and I cried all my bitterness away.*

———

> *My father abused me verbally, physically, and sexually. After years of struggle, I have finally finished my master's in counseling and am ready to help others. Recently someone asked me how in the world, with my background, I have become what I am. That set me to thinking. In high school, my church youth sponsors were a couple who believed in me, who loved me, who treated me as a part of their family. They were the ones who*

made all the difference in the world to me. I'm in my
thirties now, and I haven't seen them for years. I found
their phone number and just called—to thank them for
their love.

It is time, within the church, to nurture one another, to learn how
to be brothers and sisters, in all purity. Because this is the body
of Christ, he can give us the right love for each other, holy
love—love that mirrors his own forgiving love for us.

14
Those Who Help

Rita's Story

It was really the problems in my relationship with my husband that made me seek help. I blamed all my problems on the incest in my past. I blamed all his problems on the alcoholism in his family. I started seeing a counselor about the alcohol problem. And I noticed something: The more I talked, the better I felt.

The counseling center I was attending had a whole weekend seminar on alcoholism. Among the speakers was a psychologist who spoke about incest. I just started crying, trying to hide the tears so no one would see my response. I made the decision then, *I'm going to talk about this*. So I went to see him after the session, and he referred me to an incest therapy group.

I was in an incest therapy group for six months. And during that time, I did a lot of work on my feelings about Mom. Being a mother myself helped. It became a matter of deciding whether we were going to carry on our relationship as it was—cold and distant—or whether I could accept the way she was, the way she is, and the way she may always be, and love her anyhow. I feel I have been able to forgive her; and while I am still not really open with her, as open as I would like to be, we are getting closer.

Group therapy was so helpful for me that I went on and

trained to become a group leader. As much as one-on-one counseling can do, it seems very important to be sitting with other women who are saying things that you don't know how to put into words. You find out that there are others who have experienced what you have. It ends the feeling of isolation, the feeling that nobody has gone through what I have gone through or felt what I feel.

The most important thing that therapy gave me was a sense of hope, the confidence that my incestuous past did not have to control my whole life. It helped me to come to a kind of acceptance of my past and also to a point of taking responsibility for my future.

Let's face it. It happened. I still think of it. I still have the odd flashback and an occasional flood of memories. Last summer, I visited a house that we had lived in with Gus, and I didn't think I could go in. But I went in, and it was really dramatic the way it unlocked frozen memories. It was, at the time, very painful. It took me a good week to get over it and to talk about it. But I think it freed me a little more.

I know that some people are nervous about secular counseling groups. But I think that God puts people in our paths to help us move toward him. I have worked through a lot of things in the group that I still couldn't talk to my pastor about. Recently I heard a sermon about God being all the help you need. I think the church should stop and take a look before they put down secular counselors. I agree that you need God, but you also need people. God didn't take my problems away from me. He helped me. He put the right people in my life. He is healing my relationships, but I still have to work at it.

At my church, when I mention that I work at the Sexual Assault Center, people just sort of disappear. They don't ask what I do; they don't want to know what I do. I think that pastors and all Christians have to become aware that sexual abuse happens, and it happens even in Christian homes. Certainly there are a lot of Christians who have been affected in some way by sexual abuse. We've got to quit pretending the problems are not there and start encouraging people to get the help they need.

Getting Unstuck

Psychiatrist Scott Peck states that people need therapy when they get stuck, when they find they have reached a dead end in the ongoing process of maturation. That is an excellent rule of thumb for abuse survivors as well as for those coping with the normal frustrations and abrasions of life.

If we're stuck, if we realize we have been repeating a self-destructive action, thought, or experience, then we need to seek counseling. This can come from experts in many different fields. Spiritually mature friends can often give us wise psychological advice. Pastors and church friends often exercise spiritual gifts of discernment and knowledge that are uncannily correct and insightful.

> *I do need help. I heard someone say that a person like me or anyone who has been sexually abused as a child should have counseling for it. Why? If I am a Christian, can't I go to God for the healing I need? Or is a counselor part of God's provision in the healing process?*

The difficulty with the ruggedly individualistic John Wayne complex ("I can handle this by myself") is that it is often a smoke screen for plain old pride—a refusal to admit to ourselves or to the world that we have a problem, that we *can't* handle this by ourselves. While hundreds of people can testify that God himself met them at a point of desperate need, when they were utterly alone with no one to turn to, there are also thousands who testify that their spiritual, psychological, and emotional development was enhanced by others they trusted who held them accountable, who disciplined and encouraged them in their growth.

The human journey into maturation seems to be a rich accumulation of differing experiences—God alone in the desert places of our lives, the touch of other human hands lifting us when we have fallen, our giving to others from our own experiences with God, and our giving back some of the love we have received from others to people who are in desperate need.

We all get stuck in our developmental process. Our human ability to create defense mechanisms that hide a painful truth from ourselves so that we can go on with our lives without having to deal with it, is very efficient. A good counselor knows this is a major task: to help victims face the truth they have hidden deep inside.

In the book *Vital Lies, Simple Truths: The Psychology of Self-Deception and Shared Illusions,* Daniel Goleman discusses the dynamics of our truth-filtering system. In order to avoid the pain with which we don't have the resources to cope, in order to avoid the panicky, humiliating anxiety created by circumstances beyond our control, our subconscious filters out the experience. This creates the proverbial blind spot, the mind actively shielding itself from anxiety, censoring information to provide a sense of security.[1] A major example of this for the abuse victim is the ability of the subconscious mind to choose to forget. Several women we know have had sudden surprising memories surface when they were older, memories of their incestuous pasts—all of which had been totally blocked from the conscious mind.

The counselor's work is to help us see through our own rationalizations, our denials, and our projections, our isolating of feelings from events, our selective repressions. The healthy, truth-loving mind can do this work for itself. However, when a human being has grown into adulthood without an emphasis on truth, without facing reality as it is rather than as she wishes it to be, without coming to terms with the natural bent toward self-deception, self-awareness is much more difficult.

The survivors of child sexual abuse are often raised in an atmosphere of untruth, and consequently many have not achieved the resources for ongoing development. Emotional development has been severely disrupted, and victims often feel chained by their childhood circumstances. They feel they have nowhere to go and nothing worth living for. When the abuse has occurred during early childhood, the establishment of trust both in oneself and in others has been short-circuited. When the abuse has occurred during adolescence, social and relational skills are often arrested.

Approximately 20 percent of the victims who have faced early childhood molestations seem to show no long-range aftereffects. How wonderful that these people don't seem to need help! However, in many cases of child sexual abuse, the ability to cope is so severely damaged that a good counselor is very often part of God's provision in the healing process.

> *Having been sexually abused by my father, . . . you can imagine some of the difficulty that I've experienced throughout my life. For the past three years, I've been seeing a psychologist, and she has helped me tremendously to understand and change certain behaviors which may have resulted from this abuse. However, I must give credit where credit is due—that is to God, who is the source of all wisdom and healing. He has given me so much insight, and I am very thankful to him. . . . My psychologist is not a Christian, so it has been a little difficult to tie the mental, physical, and spiritual together in this process.*

> *Even though I thought I had "gotten over it" and no one else knew about it, the scars were there, and it finally had to come out. I finally sought counseling with a Christian psychotherapist for marital difficulties. . . . The counseling proved to be the turning point in my life. I was able to talk about the past and even in sessions with my husband to relate to him my experience. My husband was wonderful, and I worked through my anger and bitterness at my father which had carried over to my husband.*

> *Just this year, our Lord got me into therapy and into an incest group. For the first time, I am acknowledging the intense emotions that refuse to stay stuffed down, and I am wading through each memory. All that to say this: I need spiritual prayer and guidance.*

Real help can be found at two levels:

1. *Informal counseling.* This can come through friends, others who have experienced and are recovering from abuse, and/or prayer partners. Preferably, such counsel should be

sought from a sympathetic, mature person with some prior experience in helping abuse victims sort through their various concerns. An untrained person with a gift for asking astute questions that demand honest answers is also invaluable. A personal, insistent *Why?* can force victims to consider issues they normally refuse to recognize.

2. *Professional counseling.* Therapists with various specialties can help with the overall understanding of the problems experienced by abuse victims. People with special skills might include:

- Sexual assault or crisis center counselors. These people have specialized training and experience in post-assault psychological problems. They will often invite the person into a survivor's support group, one of the most effective means for dissipating the sense of aloneness which haunts many survivors. Many of the people behind the voices we quote gratefully point to these groups as vital in their initial steps toward healing.
- Pastoral counselors. Although in the past many pastors were inadequately prepared to deal with the specifics of sexual abuse consequences, a wise and discerning pastoral counselor with some training can have both the spiritual and psychological resources for helping the person who is dealing with abuse history. The pastor may also be able to provide a referral to psychologists or other trained counselors in the local area if in-depth therapy seems desirable.

  Often, the male professional minister overlooks the valuable tools at his disposal that can give enormous relief to the abuse survivor. He represents a male authority figure, a representative of Christ. He can hear private, confidential confession; he can administer Communion, which, when offered as a sacrament, may bring healing and give comfort; he can perform the laying on of hands—all of which have significance for the victims of abuse.
- Psychologists. Specially trained in the dynamics of

human interactions, psychologists are skilled in asking questions that will lead survivors into healing insights. Christian psychologists who integrate spiritual and scriptural elements are particularly beneficial to those who interpret life within a Christian frame of reference.

- Psychiatrists. Trained first in medicine, psychiatrists help severe personality disorders (which may be complicated by chemical or physical imbalances), or personality disintegration (which manifests itself in prolonged depression, schizophrenia, or psychosomatic illness). Sometimes a psychiatrist and a psychologist form a beneficial therapy team.

With all these avenues of help to choose from, it is important for the survivor to remember that she has the right to shop for the right counseling. Survivors typically do not feel that they have the right to make any demands. But they have, and must assert, the right to find someone they can trust.

Rita, the young woman whose story we have followed in the past few chapters, says this: "The person seeking help should be honest with her counselor about her Christian convictions, not being afraid to tell where she stands. The counselor will respect that position. I couldn't have talked with my pastor—I still couldn't. I think God puts people (like those at the Sexual Assault Center) at his disposal for his purposes. But certainly the abuse survivor has the right to a counselor with whom she feels comfortable."

When to Seek Psychiatric Help

Psychiatric intervention may be needed when an individual is characterized by:

1) intense anxiety, either generalized or focused (phobias, obsessions, etc.)
2) depression or anxiety of crippling intensity—preventing the person from coping with normal life
3) any of the above when coupled with physical symptoms
4) feelings of unreality, of losing a grip on reality.

Psychiatric care combines counseling and medication. Modern psychiatric medication can be a major contributor to restored health.

The Need for Hope

In her book *Door of Hope*, Jan Frank g
pursue professional counseling. First, it kee
countable; a counselor can ensure that she doe
painful work necessary for healing. Second, cou
her the objective insight she needs.[2]

Most important of all, a counselor, whether as a fr
confidante or as a professional therapist, can offer to the
survivor what she most needs: hope. Hope that her past
not ruin the rest of her life. Hope that she can break the chair
of abuse and walk freely in the present. Hope that the cycle
of pain need not be repeated in another generation.

How much counseling will be needed?

Again, this depends on the complexity of one's defense
mechanisms in conjunction with the past circumstances. Many
people simply refuse to engage in the therapeutic process.
They want a sympathetic ear, but they don't want to do any
work. The rule of thumb for getting counsel is, "When you're
stuck, get help." To evaluate therapy, ask, "Have I grown?
Have I made progress in the last three months?" If there is
no progress (if you're stuck again), either you are not cooperating significantly or your counselor doesn't have the ability
to move you along.

While it is true that some survivors find healing without
professional counseling (as Kathy did through her study of
Scripture and the support of her prayer partner—and also because of her knowledge as a psychiatric nurse), many will
need help at some point in life. The three critical times in the
life of a sexual abuse survivor when counseling is most needed
are: (1) immediately after the abuse events; (2) at the time of
marriage; and (3) when her own children near the age at which
she experienced abuse. Other major life transitions such as
the birth of a child, divorce, severe illness or medical procedures, the death of the abuser—or even positive events like a
promotion or graduation—can trigger memories and symptoms of the childhood abuse.[3]

For most survivors, the therapeutic process is painful because the past she would like to forget is confronted and
claimed.

, but oh, it hurts so much!
tian counselor. . . . I know
eal with this painful issue
care.

touch with anesthetized
es of the past in order
their lives. The long-
he child sexual abuse
it is healed, and it
en) focus.

comfortably to the present without
ow up its dark shadow, when she no longer
a victim but can grow and expand as a normal human
being (with both negative and positive emotions), when she's
glad that she's a woman, when she can eagerly embrace the gift
of each day and turn her face toward the radiant light of Christ,
she has been helped to step out of the confining, crippling effects
of a sexually abused past. At last, she can get on with life.

That is help worth finding from whatever source available.

Something You Can Do Right Now

If you are an abuse survivor, you may feel very alone in the healing process.
Think of the most loving person you know. Take a few moments (now or
over a period of days) and read the following prayer as though it came
from that loving person's heart and mouth.

My Lord Jesus,
You were wounded for each one of us.
May the blood from your wounds be poured like a healing
    ointment into the wounds of this person I love.
May this person experience cleansing, release, freedom from
    bondage, great new life—and finally joy!
I have great faith that you will answer this prayer
    because I know that it is your deepest desire.
I love you, wounded Healer.
Be health now for my friend.
In Christ's name, Amen.

If you are a friend or helper to an abuse survivor, you may pray this prayer
for the person for whom you care.

15
Turning Wounds into Ministry

Kathy's Story

It has been several years now since that day when I received—and gave—forgiveness. It has been a long time since I first heard those whispered words, "Be still and know that I am God." Now I know that he is God, *my God.*

That day was a starting point, the beginning of freedom from the prison of anger and hate and guilt in which I had lived. The years since then have been years of growth. As I have studied the Word of God, I have come to know my God, and in knowing him I can see the positive—yes, even know the reason why he allowed me the pain of this childhood experience.

My times of study became daily appointments with God, when God met with me through his Spirit and revealed to me his truth. Through the Scriptures, I have learned that my God is omniscient: he knows all (Psalm 139:1-6); he knew all about what happened to me and he knew how I felt. I saw that my God is omnipotent: he possesses all power (Job 42:2); he could have prevented what happened to me, but he didn't. Could there be a purpose? I was beginning to see. My God is omnipresent: he is everywhere (Proverbs 15:3); he saw the evil; he was there with me, yet he allowed it to happen. I also

learned that my God is incomprehensible, beyond the understanding of man (Isaiah 55:8-9). We may not always understand the purpose of the tragedies in our lives, but he does,
because he sees everything—from beginning to end.

I also came to see that my God is a God of love (1 John
4:8). A God of love who allows this to happen to a little child?
Oh, yes. I can see the depth of his love for me. I can see the
price he paid for my sin. And I also see the price he paid for
the sins of the one who sinned against me. I learned, too, that
my God is holy, righteous, just. He is merciful—an actively
compassionate being. My God is long-suffering. My God is
wise and good. My God is faithful. And yes, my God is wrath-
ful. There is within God a hatred for all that is unrighteous.

But perhaps most important to me was the truth that God
is *sovereign*. What does that mean? It means that God is totally, supremely, and preeminently reigning over all his creation (Daniel 4:35). In times of personal tragedy, we cannot
say to God, "What have you done?" He is God and we are
his creation. We don't have the right to question those things
that he has allowed. I believe that God was and is totally,
supremely, and preeminently over my life and over your life
as well (Isaiah 45:5-7). If we know and accept God as being
sovereign, we know that all situations are filtered through his
fingers of love. Absolutely nothing can touch us unless God
allows it (Romans 8:28).

Recently, I found myself thrown into the company of my
abuser through family circumstance. While I cannot say he
will ever be my favorite person, I can say with great joy that
I felt no fear, no hatred, no anger. He, the person who shadowed my life for so long, has absolutely no power over me
anymore. I am free!

What about regrets? I have none. I have seen that the abuse
I experienced was allowed by a sovereign God for purposes
of his own, purposes greater than I could have formed for
myself. Only recently, I have found the answer to my lifelong
question, "Why?"

You may not all find the answers to *your* why questions. I
remember Dr. Helen Roseveare telling the story of how she
was beaten and brutally raped by rebel soldiers. God spoke

to her at that time and asked simply, "Will you trust me, even if I never tell you why?" Sometimes we must simply affirm that kind of trust.

But I did find an answer to my why, and I found it as I have found most of the important discoveries of my new life—in Scripture. In Isaiah 61, the prophet describes the ministry of reconciliation which would be exercised by the Lord Jesus in his earthly ministry:

> The Spirit of the Sovereign Lord is on me,
> because the Lord has anointed me
>   to preach good news to the poor.
> He has sent me to bind up the brokenhearted,
>   to proclaim freedom for the captives
>   and release from darkness for the prisoners, . . .
> to comfort all who mourn,
>   and provide for those who grieve in Zion—
> to bestow on them a crown of beauty
>   instead of ashes,
> the oil of gladness
>   instead of mourning,
> and a garment of praise
>   instead of a spirit of despair.
> They will be called oaks of righteousness,
>   a planting of the Lord
>   for the display of his splendor.
> (Isaiah 61:1-3)

As a child of God, I have been given this ministry as well. It is my joy to bring hope to others who are still imprisoned by their pasts. It is my privilege to live as evidence that God is able to "make all things new" in the life of one who trusts him. The purpose of all this? "The display of God's splendor"—in my life and in the lives of all those he touches and heals.

As Kathy tells this last segment of her ongoing story, there is joy in her voice. She has been set free from her past. She has been cleansed of its defilement. And she is being used as an instrument of God's grace in the lives of others. For just such a conclusion, our voices yearn:

> *I wish you could tell me about a book where I could find stories of abuse survivors like myself who are living victorious and fruitful lives.*

> *Is there any hope that God could use me? I have such a struggle to feel "fit for the Master's use."*

The joyful truth is that God is able not only to heal but also to release the abuse survivor into fruitful, effective living. The circle of ministry may be the family, or the workplace, or the local church fellowship. Some will feel a special urgency to reach out to others who, like themselves, have lived under the long shadow of sexual abuse. Others will be eager to forget that past completely and minister Christ's love by being an effective mother, a good wife, a caring colleague, or a skilled professional.

The whole range of ministry—the opportunity to use personal spiritual gifts—lies open before the person who has experienced, and is experiencing, healing. "You were washed, you were sanctified, you were justified in the name of the Lord Jesus Christ and by the Spirit of our God" (1 Corinthians 6:11), the Bible says. Cleansed. Set apart for service. Made perfectly right in God's eyes. The hymn writer Henry Lyte puts it this way:

> Praise, my soul, the King of heaven,
> To his feet thy tribute bring;
> Ransomed, healed, restored, forgiven,
> Who, like me, his praise should sing?
> Alleluia! Alleluia!
> Praise the everlasting King![1]

Spheres of Ministry

Our spheres of ministry can be like concentric circles. The

bull's eye, or center circle, is ministry to those closest to us: our families. The next circle is ministry within our local church fellowship (a Sunday school class that needs a teacher? a nursing home visitation program that needs a volunteer?). The third circle is ministry within our community. Ask Jesus the same question as the young lawyer did in Luke 10:29, "Lord, who is my neighbor?" We have learned that "my neighbor" is *the person near me right now whose needs I am able to meet.*

Women have often told us of their desire to minister. But somehow, they often think of it as something they have to do "out there." With a shrug, they indicate the mini-audience of family or classroom or close friends, and say, "I think I was made to reach a bigger audience than this." Remember the scriptural principle: faithful in little, ruler over much. Meeting family needs, listening and being a friend, loving the unlovely and forgotten—these are significant ministries in God's sight.

Caring for Others Who Have Been Abused

Those who have experienced child abuse are very often deeply empathetic and compassionate toward suffering children and adults with similar experiences. Ministering from the healing of God is often a very natural extension of the grace that has been received. Here are some of the ministry fronts where people who have experienced substantial healing can take their places.

1. *Sharing the Good News of Healing.* As the extent of the problem of child abuse becomes generally known, we must realize that there are simply not enough professional or pastoral counselors to go around. People will have to minister to each other, sharing with the next person the comfort they have received in their distress. As one person tells his/her story, others begin to admit their needs in the same area, and healing is shared.

2. *Heightening Awareness in the Church.* People who have experienced child abuse may become the conscience of the church. Setting up a committee to find out how and where the church should minister to children and adults in the area of abuse would be a starting point. People with the gift of ad-

ministration are needed here to form structures where, within a context of Christian love and care and using a biblical view of humanity and God, people can find help. People in pastoral ministries need to be trained in detecting and helping people confront the problem of abuse. Support groups for survivors could be set up.

The church ministry should not overlook the trauma of the mother in many incestuous situations, and the need of the perpetrator to take responsibility for his sin and to seek to make amends. Finally, the church could organize efforts to fight pornography and other cultural images of male sexual violence.[2]

3. *Promoting Awareness in Legislatures.* Much needs to be done to make lawmakers aware of the long-term effects of child abuse. A beginning has been made here, but legislators still seem to draw back from creating laws with real bite— laws that would make the punishment commensurate with the damage inflicted by the crime. There needs to be careful thought as to how society can best respond to the problem of violence—and especially sexual violence—against children. Christians who have been wounded and healed may be the best spokespersons for the cause of justice in this neglected area.

A Word of Caution

As abuse survivors seek to turn their woundedness into hope and healing for others, there are several cautions to be kept in mind. First of all, survivors should not try to minister in this area too soon. They will feel passion and compassion, but may not be emotionally strong enough to cope with the added pressure of carrying others' burdens until they have had some experience of living in the light.

For many, initial ministry might be simply sharing in the ordinary church context, rebuilding relationships at home or in the workplace, growing in understanding of God and self. In considering any kind of ministry opportunity, survivors need to think through some of these questions:

- Will this kind of ministry enhance or imperil the

emotional stability I have now achieved, either
through reopening painful areas of memory or
through physical and/or mental pressure?

- Will this kind of ministry enhance or imperil the
gains that I have made in building better relationships
with others? Will it have a positive or negative
impact on my family life?

- Will this kind of ministry enhance or imperil the
prayer life that I have established as a lifeline? Will
there still be time for Bible study/reading and for
prayer, or will there be the danger of time constraints
cutting me off from the sustenance needed for vital
Christian living?

In Henry van Dyke's classic tale, *The Story of the Other Wise
Man,* the character Artaban considered whether he should use
his last gem to ransom a slave girl or whether he should save
it to give to the long-sought King. Artaban wondered, "Was
it his great opportunity or his last temptation?"[3]

We, too, have to learn to distinguish between opportunity
and temptation. More than once we have pondered urgent re-
quests to speak or help from some group or another, recognizing this dilemma. Author Colleen Townsend Evans
provides encouragement in this regard. There are seasons in
our lives, she observes, and each season has its opportunities
and its limitations. "What might be a suitable ministry for one
season might be totally unsuitable for another," she reminds
women, recalling her own overextension as a young mother
and minister's wife. "I realize now I was trying to do too
much, taking on ministries suitable for a later season too soon,
and so I was fatigued and off-balance."[4]

There is yet another caution to be heeded before we hurry
into ministry. This warning is sounded by the writer of Hebrews: "See to it . . . that no bitter root grows up to cause
trouble and defile many" (Hebrews 12:15). If there is a sliver
of unforgiveness left in our hearts, a residual anger that still
smolders, the "root of bitterness" is likely to hinder our ministry. We have all, perhaps, heard people speak about a painful
past in such a way that the message seems to be a kind of

revenge. Public statements can become a way to strike back at a family that failed to protect or at a church that failed to respond. A truly healing ministry cannot be exercised except by those whose wounded hearts have known the healing oil of the Spirit of God.

Whom Shall I Tell? How Much Shall I Tell?

We have talked about the importance of claiming the pain-filled past in words—either orally or through a journal. But one must be careful about "going public" with the story of a painful or sordid past. (You will notice that those voices who have spoken in this book have been carefully made anonymous—for reasons that might be important to all survivors.) Some of the questions that need to be answered before a story is told beyond person-to-person sharing are these:

- Who may be hurt if I tell this story now? What about my parents? my brothers and sisters? my children? Is the possibility of deep hurt within my inner family circle worth the potential ministry?
- Does my husband feel fully comfortable with my declaration of this as my past, or would he be more comfortable if I were to keep this a private matter? Since misunderstanding here will be reflected in your total relationship, don't be too quick to assume that because you feel healed of the past, your husband has fully dealt with his anger and pain.
- How fully am I healed? If there is still healing to be done, it might be better to "be still and know God" for a while longer.

Remembering that the first task of life is to build healthy and healing relationships in our own personal circles of love, the survivor can ask simply, "Dear Lord, what ministry do you wish to flow from my healed wounds? As life has flowed to me from the healed wounds of my Savior, so may hope flow to others from my own cleansed and healed wounds."

We shouldn't hurry or feel pressured into a ministry or activity by some kind of false guilt. Rather, we should move steadily, quietly in the easy yoke into which our Lord invites us (Matthew 11:28-30). May we all find opportunity to serve our Lord, our brothers and sisters, and those around us who do not yet know Christ's healing touch.

There is one more story we want to share with you. We've saved it for last. To tell it, we introduce another friend.

16
Behold, I Make All Things New

Margaret's Story

"Margaret" is the kind of woman you would like to know: attractive, poised, articulate. In her work overseas, she communicates in three languages, works comfortably with government officials or tribal leaders, and has a firsthand knowledge of international affairs. She is a grandmother many times over and is concerned with the growing families of her children. She has been involved in relief efforts for people displaced by warfare. Whether teaching in a tribal village or a graduate program in a university, she is clearly a person who knows and uses her gifts. Margaret is the epitome of fruitful, meaningful womanhood, and she shares her story here as a sign of hope for abuse survivors.

I was about five when my father first began to fondle me. When he began to have sex with my older sister when she was nine, I was terrified that it would happen to me—which, of course, it did. From the time I was nine until I was thirteen, my father used me as a sexual partner. I thought that if my sister and I kept him satisfied, perhaps he would not bother our younger sisters. But in time he got to them as well.

My parents quarreled a great deal, and my mother and all

of us children were battered and bruised in my father's violent outbursts. Much as we feared his anger when he was drunk, we feared even more his fury when, at some small provocation, he flared into a rage and beat us when he was sober.

His violence was backed up with threats of using a revolver he had come to own during a period as a police officer. We knew it was there and never doubted that he might use it. One terrible night he did, shooting my mother through the abdomen and very nearly killing her. He was arrested for attempted murder, and my mother was taken by ambulance to the hospital.

For many weeks we did not hear from either of our parents. My older sister and I, then fourteen and thirteen, cared for the four younger children the best we could, subsisting through a long summer on our twenty-acre farm. When my mother finally recovered sufficiently to make some decisions, she worked out a plea-bargaining deal whereby she would not press criminal charges. My father, in return for this, was to give her custody of the children and make support payments.

My father was released from jail and immediately married a woman with whom he had been unfaithful to my mother—a woman whose daughters he would subsequently abuse.

My mother and we six children moved to another part of the state to pick up the pieces of our lives. My mother worked full-time to care for the family, my father never contributing anything at all to our support. She came home day after day, tired to the bone. I realize now how frayed she must have felt, but no matter how hard my sisters and brother and I tried to please her—with an especially good meal or a freshly cleaned house—she seemed only aware of the one thing left undone. She was never appreciative and always critical, leaving me feeling very unsure of myself throughout my adult life.

My sister escaped the family situation by finding another home in which to live while she went to high school. But I stayed on with Mother, caring for my younger brother and sisters, leaving time for only the academic aspect of school.

We had begun to attend church when we moved. At first, my mother felt too keenly the stigma of her divorce (in those days a real scandal) and did not come with us. Later she began to enter into the life of the church. Our family's past was known, however, and I can recall that some families actually withdrew their children from the youth choir when I joined. In general, though, we found more acceptance in the church than anywhere else in that town.

The one place where I succeeded was school. My grades were good, despite frequent absenteeism to help care for children at home. I set myself a liberation time line: After graduation from high school, I decided firmly, I would leave home and go to college. I had, from very early childhood, been working out a plan whereby my life could be different from my parents' and the life of my children different from my own abused and ashamed childhood.

I remember one high school English teacher in particular who treated me with respect and made me feel that I was, in some way, worthwhile. I especially remember her inviting me to her home—a very important affirmation to me.

After two years of college, I married a boy I had met while I was in high school and who, despite his parents' objections, loved me. The summer we were married, while he was a student minister, we had a definite conversion experience in which we came to understand the meaning of the death of Christ on our behalf and claimed his death as the basis of our salvation.

Although we had been good "church kids," we had not previously had the experience of the indwelling Christ. This new faith dynamic set us alight. We met with other Christians for fellowship, studied the Bible, and prayed with a new sense of relatedness to God. Gradually, while studying at a Christian college, we became aware of a desire to commit ourselves to foreign missions.

Meanwhile, our family began to arrive. Throughout my first pregnancy I struggled with excessive nausea, which I now attribute to anxiety about what kind of mother I would be. But I had from early childhood thought through, "When I am a mother, I will do . . ." and, "I won't ever do this . . ."

I was determined to break the cycle of abuse, and by God's grace, I have. With a large family all grown, all married, all loving and serving God, I can reassure other anxious-hearted abuse survivors that *the cycle can be broken*. The pain does not have to be passed on.

Raising children in another culture has been a rugged, rich, and rewarding experience, despite the distance from medical and educational facilities. I have experienced substantial healing, but it has not been without pain. I have learned that even when I thought I had dealt with the past, there are times when I must offer forgiveness again. Memories arise unbidden and must be dealt with. "How often should I forgive my brother?" Peter asked Jesus. Jesus answered, "Seventy times seven." That tells me that forgiveness must be offered as many times as the hurtful memory arises.

My constant need for affirmation has sometimes been difficult within our marriage. My husband, while strongly supportive and loving, is not tremendously verbal about it. We have needed help and counseling to get through some hard places. But through it all, my husband has been my therapist, and Jesus, my healer.

I suspect the process of such healing may last the rest of my life. But I can truly say that I am being healed.

Margaret's story affirms that an abusive past need not be a burden, coloring the present, shadowing the future. There is much need for hope and healing in the lives of child sexual abuse victims and abusers—the kind of hope Christ can give; healing so that the cycle of abuse will not be repeated in the lives of children or others the abuse survivor loves. The chains of the past *can* be broken. The abuse survivor can walk freely into the future—with God's help.

For Kathy, the real cleansing of her pain-filled past came with the recognition of the sovereign power and purposes of her God. It was through her understanding of God's sovereignty as portrayed in the Scriptures—his ability to bring good out of evil—that she came to a place of rest.

Margaret also recognized God's sovereign power in her life—power that continues to heal the scars. She also recalls many circumstances where helpers were essential in her healing process (the high school teacher who showed a special interest, marriage counselors).

Many of our voices speak of the importance of Christian community in fostering healing and building healthy relationships with the survivor and abuser. We, as Christ's church, need to realize that adult survivors and child abusers do need our support—as a group, as families, and as individuals.

We urge you to get involved. There are many organizations that need assistance in fighting the evil of child sexual abuse—government organizations, church programs, counseling programs, volunteer programs. Or you could start your own. What about your neighbors? the callous man, the shy woman, the fearful child down the block who desperately needs a friend? They all need someone to listen, hold them accountable, and with the Spirit's help, open that door of healing in their damaged souls.

God calls us all—each with varied talents and resources—to act as instruments of his grace in the lives of others. As a community of caring, concerned Christians, we have a responsibility to minister to each other. And as Christ's healing flows through you and cleanses your wounds, so let it flow through you to others who are hurting. For all those who are wounded, that is indeed a tremendous hope for healing.

Appendix A:
Where Do We Go from Here?

Moving from ignorance or denial to determined action is a kind of "pilgrim's progress" for each of us. (See Appendix Figure 1, and see where you are on this journey.) Many who have read this book will be asking: "What can I do?" The list of ideas below can help you find your own personal starting point in confronting and combating the evil of child sexual abuse.

If You Are a Survivor:
1. Work through the self-help sections of this book thoroughly.
2. Find someone to share your story with.
3. Seek counseling. If none is available, contact your minister and ask that the church move to meet this need.
4. Become a member of an abuse survivors group, or form one with the help of a counselor with some training in this kind of therapy.
5. Begin personal Bible study and prayer.
6. Help one other abuse survivor.

If You Are a Helping Friend:
1. Share this book with your friend or neighbor who has a past history of abuse. Offer to work through it with him/her.
2. See what counseling services are available in your area.
3. Take some basic sexual assault counseling training if such is available in your area.
4. Urge your church, women's group, and Christian Education committee to plan programs to help survivors.

If You Are a Church Leader:
1. Become thoroughly informed about child sexual abuse, particularly within the Christian community.
2. Assess the needs of your congregation and community with regard to both prevention and therapy.
3. Educate your Christian Education personnel (Sunday school teachers and youth workers) in the detection and counseling of children who have been sexually (or otherwise) abused.

4. Work with local agencies such as Sexual Assault Centers to develop awareness of the problem within your congregation and community.
5. Assess the counseling resources of your church and community. Could you provide better services with better training? How could that be arranged?
6. Extend your concern to other areas of family violence.
7. Consider the ways that theological assumptions are used to justify/cover up child sexual abuse. What can you do in teaching/preaching/family life support programs to correct mis1conceptions about male dominance exercised through power within the family?
8. Form a committee including one or more abuse survivors to inform the church about this growing problem. Suggest strategies for meeting the needs of family members who are involved in some way with child sexual abuse. Include both perpetrator and victims.

For more information, contact:

Child Abuse and Neglect Clearinghouse
P.O. Box 1182
Washington, DC 20013
(800) 394-3366

Hope for the Abused
260 Guelph Street
P.O. Box 74027
Georgetown, Ontario L7G 5L1
Canada
(905) 873-6447

Appendix A

Appendix A: Figure 1
The "pilgrim's progress" to determined action

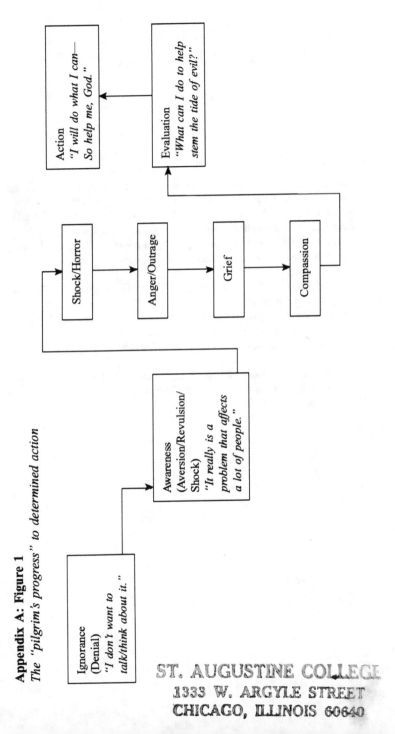

Appendix B:
What about False Accusation?

This book is premised on the understanding that survivors are telling the truth and should be believed unless there are strong grounds for disbelief. We are also aware that "false memories" are sometimes stirred up and false accusations of abuse—through malice or mistake—are sometimes made.

The following books contain some helpful resources for church leaders, counselors, and friends with regard to these troubling situations.

The "Addendum" in *Door of Hope* by Jan Frank (Nashville: Thomas Nelson Publishers, 1995).

The Myth of Repressed Memory by Elizabeth Loftus and Katharine Ketcham (New York: St. Martin's Press, 1994).

Suggestions of Abuse by Michael Yapco (New York: Simon and Schuster, 1994).

Unchained Memories by Lenore Terr (New York: Basic Books, 1994).

The "Prologue" to *The Wounded Heart* by Dan B. Allender (Colorado Springs: NavPress, 1995).

Appendix C
Prayers and Litanies

In her book *Sexual Abuse in Christian Homes and Churches,* Carolyn Holderread Heggen presents a whole chapter of prayers, litanies, and liturgies to be used in worship for child sexual abuse survivors and their spiritual communities. We've included some of these here.

Even if you are struggling spiritually, take the time to read and pray through these three examples, opening your heart in new ways to God's healing love. You may want to pray through these with a close friend or suggest them to your pastor to be used in corporate worship.

Psalm of Blessing
by Joyce Munro

You can trust your journey through darkest night,
    for you have light!

God's tenderness surrounds you
    and you are not alone.
You are making your way to the waters of peace,
    and you can ask for help along the journey.
Even though you walk through the valley of deep pain,
    you need not be afraid.
Anger salves the raw wound, and
    tears must flow to cleanse.

In the presence of your enemies,
May healers anoint you with oil,
Friends spread a table before you,
    and offer you rest;
May God bathe you in stillness,
    breathe with you,
    murmuring comfort
    in the hour when you have lost hope or strength.
For goodness and mercy belong to you
    this day and all the days of your life.

So dance joy,
>   laugh loud hallelujahs,
>   or leap hosannas.
You deserve God's peace
And shall dwell in it forever!

Affirmation of Faith
by Carolyn Holderread Heggen

Group 1:   We believe that beyond the violence,
Group 2:   there can be love;
Group 1:   That beyond the despair,
Group 2:   there can be hope;
Group 1:   That beyond the torment,
Group 2:   we will find rest;
Group 1:   That beyond our brokenness,
Group 2:   there can be healing;
Group 1:   That beyond our agony,
Group 2:   we will find joy.
All: Oh, God, transform our disbelief and gently carry us
           from darkness to light.

Litany of Commitment
by Joyce Munro

All: We commit ourselves to a world, to homes, and to churches,
           Where we attempt to weave whole cloth again—

Leader: Where those still so close to God,
           our little children,
           can weave in as high as they can reach,
           their shimmering white and gold yarns;

Men: And women lovingly restore to the cloth
           their red and purple,
           threads of their passion,
           threads of their power;

Women: And men weave in the green and orange
           of earth colors,
           all the strength of their tears,
           their tenderness in them;

Men: And from those cast aside
              for lack of perfect bodies, articulate minds,
              the weaving in of rainbow yarn
              for their deep capacity to have hope;

Women: And from those who have used
              their power wrongly,
              but have changed—
              pink for creativity,
              yellow for transformation.

Men and Women over Sixty:
              Let us elders and crones bring ancient hues
              to the weaving cloth—
              brown, rose, and violet—
              our sense of all that will pass,
              our sense of all that will come;

Women: While we who have had our boundaries of self ravaged,
              let us add stunning black,
              our color dignifying the others;

Teens and Children:
              Let this whole cloth include
              that which is not always known as thread—
              feathers,
              grass,
              seeds, and
              fur
              for resplendent mystery that is each living thing.

Leader: And let us ask the great I AM
              who intuits each heart,
              who knows star space,
              to draw blue through the warp
              blessing upon blessing
              blue upon blue,
              until there is whole cloth again.

All: (With bells, clapping, and stomping) AMEN!

Taken from *Sexual Abuse in Christian Homes and Churches* by Carolyn Holderread Heggen (Scottdale, PA: Herald Press, 1993), pp. 157-174. Used by permission.

Appendix D:
Resources

Canadian Association of Sexual Assault Centres
77 East 20th Avenue
Vancouver, BC
Canada V5V 1L7
(604) 872-8212

Child Abuse and Neglect Clearinghouse
P.O. Box 1182
Washington, DC 20013
(800) 394-3366

Family Violence and Sexual Assault Institute
1310 Clinic Drive
Tyler, TX 75701
(903) 595-6600

Hope for the Abused
260 Guelph St.
P.O. Box 74027
Gerogetown, ON
Canada L7G 5L1
(905) 873-6447

Incest Survivors Anonymous
World Service Office
P.O. Box 17245
Long Beach, CA 90807
(310) 428-5599

Incest Survivors Resource Network International
P.O. Box 7375
Las Cruces, NM 88006
(505) 521-4260

Mars Station Computer Bulletin Board
P.O. Box 038
Rockville, MD 20848
(301) 649-2347

The National Resource Center on Child Sexual Abuse
2204 Whitesburg Drive, Suite 200
Huntsville, AL 35801
(205) 534-6868

Parents United
232 E. Gish Road
San Jose, CA 95112
(408) 453-7611

Survivors of Incest Anonymous
World Service Office
P.O. Box 21817
Baltimore, MD 21222
(410) 282-3400

Voices in Action
P.O. Box 148309
Chicago, IL 60614
(800) 7-VOICE-8 or (312) 327-1500

Notes

1/The Nature of Child Sexual Abuse

1. Finkelhor, David. "Current Information on the Scope and Nature of Child Sexual Abuse," *The Future of Children,* 4 (Summer/Fall 1994), p. 34.

Gordon, Betty N. and Carolyn S. Schroeder. *Sexuality: A Developmental Approach to Problems* (New York: Plenum Press, 1995), p. 49.

2. Finkelhor, "Current Information on the Scope and Nature of Child Sexual Abuse," p. 33.

Gilmartin, Pat. *Rape, Incest, and Child Sexual Abuse* (New York: Garland Publishing, 1994), p. 18.

Whetsell-Mitchell, Juliann. *Rape of the Innocent* (Washington, DC: Taylor & Francis, 1995), p. 3.

3. Allender, Dan B. *The Wounded Heart* (Colorado Springs: NavPress, Rev. Ed. 1995), p. 49.

Finkelhor, "Current Information on the Scope and Nature of Child Sexual Abuse," p. 33.

Weiner, Neil and Sharon E. Robinson Kurpius. *Shattered Innocence* (Washington, DC: Taylor & Francis, 1995), p. 2.

4. Whetsell-Mitchell, *Rape of the Innocent,* p. 3.

5. Butler, Sandra. *Conspiracy of Silence: The Trauma of Incest* (San Francisco: New Glide Publications, 1978), p. 31.

6. Zaphiris, Alexander G. *Methods and Skills for a Differential Assessment and Treatment in Incest, Sexual Abuse and Sexual Exploitation of Children* (Denver: The American Humane Association, 1983), p. 3.

7. Allender, *The Wounded Heart,* p. 97.

8. Finkelhor, "Current Information on the Scope and Nature of Child Sexual Abuse," p. 34.

9. This estimate is still the best one. Studies vary, but so many cluster around 20% to 33% that most researchers believe that at least one in five to one in three women experienced sexual abuse as a child. Sources: Courtois, Christine. "Assessment and Diagnosis," in *Treating Women Molested in Childhood* by Catherine Classen (San Francisco: Jossey-Bass Publishers, 1995), p. 1; Finkelhor, "Current Information on the Scope and Nature of Child Sexual Abuse," p. 37; Gordon and Schroeder, *Sexuality: A Developmental Approach to Problems,* p. 48; Hall, Terese A. "Spiritual Effects of Childhood Sexual Abuse in Adult Christian Women," *Journal of Psychology*

and Theology 23 (1995), p. 129; Kinnear, Karen. *Childhood Sexual Abuse: A Reference Handbook* (Santa Barbara: ABC-CLIO, 1995), p. 127; Weiner and Kurpius, *Shattered Innocence*, p. 2; and Whetsell-Mitchell, *Rape of the Innocent*, p. 1.

10. Finkelhor, "Current Information on the Scope and Nature of Child Sexual Abuse," pp. 38-39.

Whetsell-Mitchell, *Rape of the Innocent*, p. 16.

See also Diana Russell's 1983 landmark study, which was based on a sociometrically accurate random sample of adult women and an extensive questionnaire, "The Incidence and Prevalence of Intrafamilial and Extrafamilial Sexual Abuse of Female Children," *Child Abuse and Neglect*, 7 (1983), p. 137.

11. Finkelhor, "Current Information on the Scope and Nature of Child Sexual Abuse," pp. 38-39.

12. Allender, *The Wounded Heart*, p. 92.

Weiner and Kurpius, *Shattered Innocence*, p. 2.

13. Finkelhor, "Current Information on the Scope and Nature of Child Sexual Abuse," p. 46.

Mosgofian, Peter and George Ohlschlager. *Sexual Misconduct in Counseling and Ministry* (Dallas, TX: Word, 1995), p. 123.

14. Heggen, Carolyn Holderread. *Sexual Abuse in Christian Homes and Churches* (Scottdale, PA: Herald Press, 1993), pp. 73, 83-97.

15. Butman, Richard E. "Hidden Victims: The Facts about Incest," *HIS Magazine*, April 1983.

16. For further development of the points raised in this brief discussion, see: James and Phyllis Alsdurf, *Battered Into Submission* (Downers Grove, IL: InterVarsity Press, 1989); Gretchen Gabelein Hull, *Equal to Serve: Women and Men in the Church and Home* (Old Tappan, NJ: Revell, 1987); Mary Stewart Van Leeuwen, *Gender and Grace* (Downers Grove, IL: InterVarsity Press, 1990).

2/The Physical and Emotional Aftermath

1. Forward, Susan and Craig Buck. *Betrayal of Innocence: Incest and Its Devastation* (New York: Penguin Books, 1978), p. 20.

2. Weiner and Kurpius, *Shattered Innocence*, p. 2.

Whetsell-Mitchell, *Rape of the Innocent*, p. 1.

3. Armstrong, Louise. *Kiss Daddy Goodnight: A Speak-Out On Incest* (New York: Hawthorne Books, Inc., 1978), p. 67.

4. Rush, Florence. *The Best Kept Secret: Sexual Abuse of Children* (Englewood Cliffs, NJ: Prentice-Hall, 1980), p. 195.

5. Meiselman, Karin C. *Incest: A Psychological Study of Causes and Effects with Treatment Recommendations* (San Francisco: Jossey-Bass, 1978), p. 188.

6. Allender, *The Wounded Heart*, p. 59.

7. Steele, Brandt F. and Helen Alexander. "Long-term Effects of Sexual Abuse in Childhood," in *Sexually Abused Children and Their Families* by

Patricia Beezley Mrazek and C. Henry Kempe (New York: Pergamon Press, 1981), pp. 223-233.

8. Forward and Buck, *Betrayal of Innocence,* p. 20.

9. Meiselman, *Incest: A Psychological Study of Causes and Effects,* p. 198.

10. Allender, *The Wounded Heart,* pp. 140, 166.

Gilmartin, Pat. *Rape, Incest, and Child Sexual Abuse,* p. 135.

Whetsell-Mitchell, *Rape of the Innocent,* p. 34.

11. Siemers, Mary Ellen. "Treatment Methods for Adult Female Survivors of Incest: A Review of the Literature," unpublished master's thesis, University of Wisconsin, May 1986, pp. 11-13.

12. Allender, *The Wounded Heart,* p. 67.

13. Green, Holly Wagner. *Turning Fear to Hope* (Nashville: Thomas Nelson Publishers, 1984), p. 78.

14. Allen, Charlotte Vale. *Daddy's Girl* (Toronto: McClelland and Stewart, 1980), p. 92.

3/Behavioral and Relational Problems

1. Freud, Anna. "A Psychoanalyst's View of Sexual Abuse by Parents" in *Sexually Abused Children and Their Families* by Patricia Beezley Mrazek and C. Henry Kempe (New York: Pergamon Press, 1981), pp. 33-34.

2. Finkelhor, David. *Sexually Victimized Children* (New York: The Free Press, a division of MacMillan, 1979), chapter 7.

3. Meiselman, *Incest: A Psychological Study of Causes and Effects,* p. 186.

4. Allender, *The Wounded Heart,* p. 54-55.

5. Allender, *The Wounded Heart,* p. 54.

Gilmartin, *Rape, Incest, and Child Sexual Abuse,* p. 149.

6. Steele and Alexander, "Long-term Effects of Sexual Abuse in Childhood," p. 233.

7. Densen-Gerber, Judianne. "Incest as a Causative Factor in Anti-Social Behavior: An Exploratory Study" in *Child Abuse: Where Do We Go From Here?* conference proceedings, Children's Memorial Hospital National Medical Center, February 18-20, 1977, pp. 83-88.

8. DeBoe, James. "Personality-Splitting Trauma," *Perspectives,* 7 (Sept. 1992), p. 14.

9. Meiselman, *Incest: A Psychological Study of Causes and Effects,* p. 230.

10. Forward and Buck, *Betrayal of Innocence,* p. 22.

11. Allender, *The Wounded Heart,* pp. 163-165.

Frank, Jan. *Door of Hope* (Nashville: Thomas Nelson, 1995), pp. 24-26.

12. Allender, *The Wounded Heart,* pp. 124-25.

13. Meiselman, *Incest: A Psychological Study of Causes and Effects,* p. 215.

14. Justice, Blair and Rita Justice. *The Broken Taboo: Sex in the Family* (New York: Human Sciences Press, 1979), p. 187.

15. Meiselman, *Incest: A Psychological Study of Causes and Effects,* p. 245.

16. Heggen, *Sexual Abuse in Christian Homes and Churches,* p. 136.

17. Tsai, Mavis and Nathaniel N. Wagner. "Therapy Groups for Women Sexually Molested as Children," *Archives of Sexual Behavior,* 7, no. 5 (1958), p. 424.

4/The Shadowed Spirit

1. There is more research available now on the spiritual implications of child sexual abuse. See sources: Dan Allender; Terese Hall; Carolyn Holderread Heggen; as well as Donna Kane, Sharon E. Cheston, and Joanne Greer.

2. Colson, Charles. *Who Speaks for God?* (Westchester, IL: Crossway Books, 1985), p. 31.

3. Hall, Terese A. "Spiritual Effects of Childhood Sexual Abuse in Adult Christian Women," *Journal of Psychology and Theology,* 23 (1995), p. 131.

4. Heggen, *Sexual Abuse in Christian Homes and Churches,* p. 44.

5. Forward and Buck, *Betrayal of Innocence,* p. 23.

6. Schaeffer, Francis. *The God Who Is There* (Downers Grove, IL: InterVarsity Press, 1968), p. 102.

7. White, John. *Masks of Melancholy* (Downers Grove, IL: InterVarsity Press, 1982), p. 202.

8. Meiselman, *Incest: A Psychological Study of Causes and Effects,* p. 347.

9. Heggen, *Sexual Abuse in Christian Homes and Churches,* p. 45.

5/Claiming the Past

1. Allen, *Daddy's Girl.*

2. Ricks, Chip. Preface to *Carol's Story* (Carol Stream, IL: Tyndale House Publishers, 1981).

3. Klug, Ron. "Looking Backward" in *How to Keep a Spiritual Journal* (Minneapolis: Augsburg Books, 1993).

4. Tavris, Carol. *Anger: The Misunderstood Emotion* (New York: Simon and Schuster, 1982), p. 23.

5. Tavris, *Anger: The Misunderstood Emotion,* p. 23

6. Lake, Frank. *Tight Corners in Pastoral Counseling* (Darton, Longman, and Todd, 1981), p. 137.

6/The Freedom of Forgiveness

1. Smedes, Lewis B. *How Can It Be All Right When Everything Is All Wrong?* (San Francisco: Harper & Row, Inc., 1982), p. 33.

2. Dickens, Charles. *Great Expectations* (New York: Oxford University Press, 1991), p. 82.

3. ten Boom, Corrie. *The Hiding Place* (Fleming H. Revell, 1971), p. 215.

7/The Journey toward Healing

1. Forward and Buck, *Betrayal of Innocence,* p. 166.

2. Peck, M. Scott. *The Road Less Traveled* (New York: Simon and Schuster, 1978) p. 55.

3. White, *Masks of Melancholy,* p. 202.

4. Mother Teresa. *Words to Love By* (Notre Dame: Ave Maria Press, 1983), p. 40.

8/Thinking Straight about God

1. Hancock, Maxine. *Love, Honor and Be Free* (Chicago: Moody Press, 1975), pp. 129-130.

2. Hester, Richard L. *Family Stories as Bearers of the Family's Theology* (Unpublished manuscript, 1983), pp. 88-90.

3. Tozer, A. W. *The Knowledge of the Holy* (New York: Harper and Row, 1961), p. 117.

10/Understanding the Abuser

1. Summit, Roland. "Typical Characteristics of Father-Daughter Incest: A Guide for Investigation" (Unpublished paper, n.d.), pp. 18-19.

2. Justice and Justice, *The Broken Taboo,* p. 69.

3. Heggen, *Sexual Abuse in Christian Homes and Churches,* pp. 74-75.

4. This material by Dr. Butman was originally published as an article titled "Hidden Victims: The Facts about Incest," in *HIS Magazine,* April 1983, p. 21.

5. Groth, A. Nicholas, William F. Hobson and Thomas S. Gary. "The Child Molester: Clinical Observation," in *Social Work and Child Sexual Abuse,* eds. Jon R. Conte and David A. Shore, 1982, pp. 129-144.

6. Dhawan, Sonia and W. L. Marshall. "Sexual Abuse Histories of Sexual Offenders," *Sexual Abuse: A Journal of Research and Treatment,* 8 (1996), p. 14.

Briggs, Freda and Russell Hawkins. "A Comparison of the Childhood Experiences of Convicted Male Child Molesters and Men Who Were Sexually Abused in Childhood and Claimed to be Nonoffenders," *Child Abuse and Neglect,* 20 (1996), p. 222.

7. Badgley, Robin et al. *Sexual Offenses Against Children in Canada* (Ottawa: Canadian Government Publishing Centre, 1984).

8. Dhawan and Marshall, "Sexual Abuse Histories of Sexual Offenders," p. 14.

9. Briggs and Hawkins, "A Comparison of the Childhood Experiences of Convicted Male Child Molesters and Men Who Were Sexually Abused in Childhood and Claimed to be Nonoffenders," p. 222.

10. Abel, G. G. and J. V. Becker and M. Mittleman and J. Cunningham-Rathner and J. L. Rouleau, and W. D. Murphy. "Self-Reported Sex Crimes of Non-Incarcerated Paraphilias," *Journal of Interpersonal Violence,* 2 (1987), pp. 3-35.

11. Armstrong, *Kiss Daddy Goodnight,* p. 235.

12. Summit, "Typical Characteristics of Father-Daughter Incest: A Guide for Investigation," p. 13.

13. Summit, "Typical Characteristics of Father-Daughter Incest: A Guide for Investigation," p. 15.

14. Meiselman, *Incest: A Psychological Study of Causes and Effects,* p. 180.

15. Monfalcone, Wesley R. *Coping with Abuse in the Family* (Philadelphia: The Westminster Press, 1980), pp. 72-75.

16. Summit, "Typical Characteristics of Father-Daughter Incest: A Guide for Investigation," p. 16

17. O'Brien, Shirley. *Child Pornography* (Dubuque, IA: Kendall/Hunt Publishing, 1983), p. 82.

18. Armstrong, *Kiss Daddy Goodnight,* p. 234.

19. Dhawan and Marshall, "Sexual Abuse Histories of Sexual Offenders," p. 12.

20. Briggs and Hawkins, "A Comparison of the Childhood Experiences of Convicted Male Child Molesters and Men Who Were Sexually Abused in Childhood and Claimed to Be Nonoffenders," p. 222.

21. Groth, Nicholas. *Men Who Rape: The Psychology of the Offender* (New York: Plenum Publishing Corp., 1979).

22. Mosgofian and Ohlschlager, *Sexual Misconduct in Counseling and Ministry,* p. 124.

23. Badgley, *Sexual Offenses Against Children in Canada.*

24. Cross, Theodore P., and Debra Whitcomb and Edward De Vos. "Criminal Justice Outcomes of Prosecution of Child Sexual Abuse: A Case Flow Analysis," *Child Abuse & Neglect,* 19 (1995), p. 1436.

Gray, Ellen. *Unequal Justice* (New York: The Free Press, 1993), pp. 3, 102.

25. Badgley, *Sexual Offenses Against Children in Canada.*

26. Gray, *Unequal Justice,* p. 3.

27. Marshall quoted in Scott, David Alexander. *Pornography: Its Effects on the Family, Community and Culture* (Guild of Family Protection Institute, 1984), p. 13.

28. Marshall, W. L. "The Use of Explicit Stimuli by Rapists, Child Molesters, and Nonoffender Males," *Journal of Sex Research* 25 (1988), pp. 267-288.

29. Bennett, Ralph W. and Daryl F. Gates. "The Relationship between Pornography and Extrafamilial Child Sexual Abuse," *The Police Chief* 58 (1991), p. 19.

30. Zaphiris, Alexander G. "Father-Daughter Incest" in *Sexual Abuse of Children: Implications for Treatment* (Colorado: Child Protection Division, 1983), p. 90.

11/Portrait of an Abuser

1. Justice and Justice, *The Broken Taboo,* p. 244.

2. Whetsell-Mitchell, *Rape of the Innocent,* pp. 139-140.

3. Allender, *The Wounded Heart,* p. 258.

4. Heggen, *Sexual Abuse in Christian Homes and Churches,* p. 144.

12/The Mother of the Abused

1. Jacobs, Janet Liebman. *Victimized Daughters* (New York: Routledge, 1994), pp. 26-29.

2. O'Brien, Shirley. *We Can! Combat Child Sexual Abuse* (Tucson, AZ: College of Agriculture, Univ. of Arizona, 1982), pp. 27-29.

3. Frank, *Door of Hope*, p. 193; Allender, *The Wounded Heart*, p. 54.

4. Meiselman, *Incest: A Psychological Study of Causes and Effects*, p. 219.

5. Jacobs, *Victimized Daughters*, pp. 16-23.

6. Gilmartin, *Rape, Incest, and Child Sexual Abuse*, p. 82.

7. Armstrong, *Kiss Daddy Goodnight*, p. 239.

8. Nanaimo Rape Assault Center. "Realities of Child Sexual Abuse" (Nanaimo, British Columbia, noncopyrighted mimeographed project, n.d.) pp. 51-52.

13/Renewing Relationships

1. Runions, Dr. J. Ernest, medical director, interview. Coquitlam, BC: British Columbia Hospital.

2. Freud, Sigmund. "Studies on Hysteria" in *The Best Kept Secret: Sexual Abuse of Children* by Florence Rush (Englewood Cliffs, NJ: Prentice-Hall, Inc., 1980), pp. 80ff.

3. Kinsey, Alfred C. and Wardell B. Pomeroy and Clyde E. Martin and Paul H. Gebhard. *Sexual Behavior in the Human Female* (Philadelphia: W. B. Saunders Company, 1953), p. 121.

4. Smiley, Gene. "Jesus Loves the Little Children, Black and Blue" in *The Sunday School Counselor,* vol. 44, no. 9, September 1984, p. 47.

5. Miller, Kathy Collard. *Out of Control! A Christian Parent's Victorious Struggle with Child Abuse* (Waco: Word Books 1984).

14/Those Who Help

1. Goleman, Daniel. *Vital Lies, Simple Truths: The Psychology of Self-Deception and Shared Illusions* (New York: Simon and Schuster, 1985), p. 153.

2. Frank, *Door of Hope*, p. 201.

3. Weiner and Kurpius, *Shattered Innocence*, pp. 25-26.

15/Turning Wounds into Ministry

1. Lyte, Henry F. "Praise, My Soul, the King of Heaven," copyright 1930 by G. Schirmer, Inc.

2. Heggen, *Sexual Abuse in Christian Homes and Churches*, p. 183.

3. Van Dyke, Henry. *The Story of the Other Wise Man* (London: Wyvern Books, 1961), p. 90.

4. Evans, Colleen Townsend. Verbal address at the *Women Alive!* conference, University of Waterloo, April 27, 1984.

Bibliography

Abel, G. G., and J. V. Becker and M. Mittleman and J. Cunningham-Rathner and J. L. Rouleau and W. D. Murphy. "Self-Reported Sex Crimes of Non-Incarcerated Paraphilias." *Journal of Interpersonal Violence,* 2, 1987.

Allen, Charlotte Vale. *Daddy's Girl.* Toronto: McClelland and Stewart, 1980.

Allender, Dan B. *The Wounded Heart* (Revised and Updated). Colorado Springs: NavPress, 1995.

Armstrong, Louise. *Kiss Daddy Goodnight: A Speak-Out on Incest.* New York: Hawthorne Books, Inc., 1978.

Badgley, Robin, et al. *Sexual Offenses Against Children in Canada.* Ottawa: Canadian Government Publishing Centre, 1984.

Bennett, Ralph W. and Daryl F. Gates. "The Relationship Between Pornography and Extrafamilial Child Sexual Abuse." *The Police Chief,* 58, 1991.

Briggs, Freda and Russell M. F. Hawkins. "A Comparison of the Childhood Experiences of Convicted Male Child Molesters and Men Who Were Sexually Abused in Childhood and Claimed to Be Nonoffenders." *Child Abuse and Neglect,* 20, 1996.

Butler, Sandra. *Conspiracy of Silence: The Trauma of Incest.* San Francisco: New Glide Publications, 1978.

Cross, Theodore P. and Debra Whitcomb and Edward De Vos. "Criminal Justice Outcomes of Prosecution of Child Sexual Abuse: A Case Flow Analysis." *Child Abuse and Neglect,* 19, no. 12, 1995.

DeBoe, James. "Personality-Splitting Trauma." *Perspectives,* 7, 1992.

Densen-Gerber, Judianne. "Incest as a Causative Factor in Anti-Social Behavior: An Exploratory Study" in Child Abuse: Where Do We Go From Here? conference proceedings, Children's Memorial Hospital National Medical Center, February 1977.

Dhawan, Sonia and W. L. Marshall. "Sexual Abuse Histories of Sexual Offenders." *Sexual Abuse: A Journal of Research and Treatment,* 8, no. 1, 1996.

Finkelhor, David. "Current Information on the Scope and Nature of Child Sexual Abuse." *The Future of Children,* 4, no. 2, 1994.

_____. *Sexually Victimized Children.* New York: The Free Press, a division of MacMillan Company, 1979.

Forward, Susan and Craig Buck. *Betrayal of Innocence: Incest and Its Devastation.* New York: Penguin Books, 1978 (1988 revised edition available).

Frank, Jan. *Door of Hope (Revised and Updated).* Nashville: Thomas Nelson, 1995.

Freud, Anna. "A Psychoanalyst's View of Sexual Abuse by Parents" from *Sexually Abused Children and Their Families* by P. B. Mrazek and C. H. Kempe. New York: Pergamon Press, 1981.

Gilmartin, Pat. *Rape, Incest, and Child Sexual Abuse.* New York: Garland Publishing, 1994.

Goleman, Daniel. *Vital Lies, Simple Truths: The Psychology of Self-Deception and Shared Illusions.* New York: Simon and Schuster, 1985.

Gray, Ellen. *Unequal Justice.* New York: The Free Press, 1993.

Groth, A. Nicholas. *Men Who Rape: The Psychology of the Offender.* New York: Plenum Publishing Corp., 1979.

Groth, A. Nicholas and William F. Hobson and Thomas S. Gary. "The Child Molester: Clinical Observation," in *Social Work and Child Sexual Abuse,* eds. J. R. Conte and D. A. Shore, 1982.

Green, Holly Wagner. *Turning Fear to Hope.* Nashville: Thomas Nelson Publishers, 1984.

Hall, Terese A. "Spiritual Effects of Childhood Sexual Abuse in Adult Christian Women." *Journal of Psychology and Theology,* 23, no. 2, 1995.

Heggen, Carolyn Holderread. *Sexual Abuse in Christian Homes and Churches.* Scottdale, PA: Herald Press, 1993.

Jacobs, Janet Liebman. *Victimized Daughters.* New York: Routledge, 1994.

Justice, Blair and Rita Justice. *The Broken Taboo: Sex in the Family.* New York: Human Sciences Press, 1979.

Klug, Ron. *How to Keep a Spiritual Journal.* Minneapolis: Augsburg Books, 1993.

Marshall, W. L. "The Use of Explicit Stimuli by Rapists, Child Molesters, and Nonoffender Males." *Journal of Sex Research,* 25, 1988.

Meiselman, Karin C. *Incest: A Psychological Study of Causes and Effects with Treatment Recommendations.* San Francisco: Jossey-Bass, Inc., 1978 (1992 reprint available).

Monfalcone, Wesley R. *Coping with Abuse in the Family.* Philadelphia: The Westminster Press, 1980.

Mosgofian, Peter and George Ohlschlager. *Sexual Misconduct in Counseling and Ministry.* Dallas: Word, Inc., 1995.

Nanaimo Rape Assault Center. "Realities of Child Sexual Abuse," a non-copyrighted mimeographed project. Nanaimo, British Columbia, Canada, n.d.

O'Brien, Shirley. *Child Pornography.* Dubuque, IA: Kendall/Hunt Publishing, 1983 (1992 second edition available.)

_____. *We Can! Combat Child Sexual Abuse.* Tucson, AZ: University of Arizona College of Agriculture, 1982.

Peck, M. Scott. *The Road Less Traveled.* New York: Simon and Schuster, 1978 (1993 edition by Buccaneer Books available).

Ricks, Chip. *Carol's Story.* Carol Stream, IL: Tyndale House, 1981.

Rush, Florence. *The Best Kept Secret: Sexual Abuse of Children.* Englewood Cliffs, NJ: Prentice-Hall, Inc., 1980 (1992 edition by McGraw available).

Russell, Diana. "The Incidence and Prevalence of Intrafamilial and Extra-familial Sexual Abuse of Female Children." *Child Abuse and Neglect,* 7, 1983.

Scott, David Alexander. *Pornography: Its Effects on the Family, Community and Culture.* Guild of Family Protection Institute, 1984.

Siemers, Mary Ellen. "Treatment Methods for Adult Female Survivors of Incest: A Review of the Literature." University of Wisconsin, unpublished master's thesis, May 1986.

Smiley, Gene. "Jesus Loves the Little Children, Black and Blue" in *The Sunday School Counselor,* Vol. 44, no. 9, September 1984.

Steele, Brandt F. and Helen Alexander. "Long-term Effects of Sexual Abuse in Childhood," in Mrazek, Patricia Beezley and C. Henry Kempe, *Sexually Abused Children and Their Families.* New York: Pergamon Press, 1981.

Summit, Roland. "Typical Characteristics of Father-Daughter Incest: A Guide for Investigation." Unpublished paper, n.d.

Tavris, Carol. *Anger: The Misunderstood Emotion.* New York: Simon and Schuster, 1982 (1989 edition available).

Tsai, Mavis and Nathaniel N. Wagner. "Therapy Groups for Women Sexually Molested as Children." *Archives of Sexual Behavior,* 7, no. 5, 1958.

Weiner, Neil and Sharon E. Robinson Kurpius. *Shattered Innocence.* Washington, DC: Taylor & Francis, 1995.

Whetsell-Mitchell, Juliann. *Rape of the Innocent.* Washington, DC: Taylor & Francis, 1995.

White, John. *Masks of Melancholy.* Downers Grove, IL: InterVarsity Press, 1982.

Zaphiris, Alexander G. "Father-Daughter Incest" in *Sexual Abuse of Children: Implications for Treatment.* Denver, CO: Child Protection Division, 1983.

———. *Methods and Skills for a Differential Assessment and Treatment in Incest, Sexual Abuse and Sexual Exploitation of Children.* Denver, CO: The American Humane Association, 1983.

Other Helpful Books and Articles Not Cited

Bohonos, Sybil. *Why Me, Lord?* Edmonton: Heart Communications, 1992.

Courtois, Christine. "Assessment and Diagnosis," in Classen, Catherine, *Treating Women Molested in Childhood.* San Francisco: Jossey-Bass Publishers, 1995.

Gordon, Betty N. and Carolyn S. Schroeder. *Sexuality: A Developmental Approach to Problems.* New York: Plenum Press, 1995.

Kane, Donna and Sharon E. Cheston and Joanne Greer. "Perceptions of God by Survivors of Childhood Sexual Abuse: An Exploratory Study in an Underresearched Area." *Journal of Psychology and Theology,* 21, no. 3, 1993.

Kinnear, Karen L. *Childhood Sexual Abuse: A Reference Handbook.* Santa Barbara, CA: ABC-CLIO, 1995.

Lewis, C. S. *The Problem of Pain.* New York: Simon and Schuster, 1978.

Mennen, Ferol E. and Diane Meadow. "The Relationship of Abuse Characteristics to Symptoms in Sexually Abused Girls." *Journal of Interpersonal Violence,* 10, no. 3, 1995.

Sterling, Beth. *The Thorn of Sexual Abuse.* Grand Rapids: Fleming H. Revell, 1994.

Index